护患情境会话精选 50 例

Fifty Selected Cases of Nurse-Patient Communication

主编 李惠玲 林 璐

东南大学出版社
SOUTHEAST UNIVERSITY PRESS
·南京·

图书在版编目(CIP)数据

护患情境会话精选 50 例 / 李惠玲,林璐主编. ——南京:东南大学出版社,2012.12
 ISBN 978-7-5641-3905-6

Ⅰ. ①护… Ⅱ. ①李… ②林… Ⅲ. ①护理-英语-口语 Ⅳ. ①H319.9

中国版本图书馆 CIP 数据核字(2012)第 273201 号

护患情境会话精选 50 例

出版发行	东南大学出版社
出 版 人	江建中
社　　址	南京市四牌楼 2 号(邮编:210096)
网　　址	http://www.seupress.com
责编电话	025-83790510
经　　销	全国各地新华书店
印　　刷	南京玉河印刷厂印刷
开　　本	880 mm×1230 mm　1/32
印　　张	8
字　　数	238 千字
版 印 次	2012 年 12 月第 1 版第 1 次印刷
书　　号	ISBN 978-7-5641-3905-6
印　　数	1~3000 册
定　　价	22.00 元(含光盘)

＊本社图书若有印装质量问题,请直接与营销部联系,电话:025-83791830。

护患情境会话精选 50 例
Fifty Selected Cases of Nurse-Patient Communication

名誉主编　周薇青

主　　编　李惠玲　林　璐

副 主 编　眭文洁　田　利

主　　审　(美国)吴·袁剑云　吴　捷　霍孝蓉　李　勋

审　　阅　林　璐　(美国)Steven Pieter Bol　(美国)Denise Marie Bol

朗　　读　(美国)Steven Pieter Bol　(美国)Denise Marie Bol

　　　　　王苏苏　冯婷婷　林　璐　胡晓敏

剪　　辑　林　璐　李春会

录　　制　陈　飞

责任编辑　张　慧

编委(按姓氏笔画顺序)

王玉宇	王　洁	王　莉	王　婷	王　稚	毛莉芬	方慧麟
吕金星	朱巍巍	乔美珍	刘　琦	汤文决	孙丽华	苏翠红
杨小芳	杨晓莉	吴山虹	吴玉芳	汪小华	沈梅芬	沈　琴
宋良琤	张　妍	陆敏霞	金美娟	周月丽	赵惠英	胡秀英
钮美娥	施耀方	姚文英	秦长喻	顾　兰	钱红英	徐苏丹
徐琴娟	徐　蓉	徐　颖	殷雪群	曹影婕	阐玉英	惠品晶
程　平	薛小玲					

前　　言

自从中英文对照的《护患情境会话 100 例》问世(出版)后,受到业内外人士的普遍青睐,尤其得到外国友人和境外同胞的欢迎,原因主要源于临床真实情境的再现以及英语支持,使之成为国内外同道顺达交流沟通的专业书籍,更为诸多护理院校案例教学和青年护士沟通培训提供了素材。之后曾有中华医学会电子音像出版社以动漫形式呈现于《临床实践双语教材》并荣获苏州大学教学成果一等奖殊荣。

鉴于教材的受众人群以及携带学习所需,经过编委会跟踪教材使用效果及学习者的需要,本着以读者为中心的人本理念,从原来 126 例会话案例中精选 50 例,并邀请美国专家以及护理专业英语教师、医生、临床护士重新修改并增加配音后,作为护理人员学习沟通技巧和专业英语的辅导教材,期望能够更方便护理人员学习和使用。

感谢为此书付出辛勤劳动的美国乔治梅森大学吴·袁剑云全家、美国 Steven Pieter Bol, Denise Marie Bol 夫妇以及苏大附一院相关护理同道的努力协作,将护理病人的亲身体验和对病患家庭感同身受的人文关怀情感与护理技术融为一体,构成一本真切爱至的立体教科书。点点滴滴渗透、潜移默化引导,将专业化的护理和职业化的语言以临床真实的情景呈现给读者,并加入安宁照护的人文关怀灵魂篇,达到既学语言、又学专业化护理的目标。另外,也感谢苏州广电局同道的无私帮助和支持。

在我院即将迎来 130 年华诞之际,谨以此书作为医院护理同道仁心精技、善待病家、优质护理的真情奉献。

由于配音时间较为仓促,如有不到之处敬请读者谅解包容,及时将意见反馈给主编本人或出版社,以便今后不断修正,使之更臻完善。

李惠玲
2012 年 11 月 28 日

目 录

第一部分 内科护患沟通
Part Ⅰ Medical Nursing Care

Ⅰ-1. 急诊 PTCA 病人的术前指导 ……………………………（ 3 ）
Pre-procedure Instructions for an Emergency Percutaneous Transluminal Coronary Angioplasty（PTCA）Patient

Ⅰ-2. 高血压病人的用药安全指导 ……………………………（ 8 ）
Medication Safety Instructions for a Patient with Hypertension

Ⅰ-3. "先心"病人食道超声心动图检查前的指导 ……………（ 12 ）
Instructions for a Patient with Congenital Cardiovascular Disease before a Transesophageal Echocardiogram

Ⅰ-4. 慢性心力衰竭病人的健康指导 …………………………（ 16 ）
Health Instructions for a Patient with Chronic Heart Failure

Ⅰ-5. 呼吸衰竭病人咳嗽排痰指导 ……………………………（ 19 ）
Coughing and Expectoration Instructions for a Patient with Respiratory Failure

Ⅰ-6. "肺心"病人安全用氧的指导 ……………………………（ 23 ）
Oxygen Safety Instructions for a Patient with Chronic Pulmonary Heart Disease

Ⅰ-7. 咯血病人的健康宣教 ……………………………………（ 26 ）
Health Education for a Patient with Hemoptysis

Ⅰ-8. 机械通气病人的健康指导 ……………………………（ 30 ）
　　　Health Instructions for a Patient with Mechanical Ventilation

Ⅰ-9. 消化性溃疡病人用药指导 ……………………………（ 35 ）
　　　Medication Instructions for a Patient with Peptic Ulcer

Ⅰ-10. 病毒性脑炎病人的护理援助 …………………………（ 39 ）
　　　Nursing Support for a Patient with Viral Encephalitis

Ⅰ-11. 脑神经多普勒检查情景会话 …………………………（ 43 ）
　　　Conversations during a Doppler Cerebral Ultrasonic Examination

Ⅰ-12. 胰岛素的用药指导 ……………………………………（ 57 ）
　　　Instructions on the Use of Insulin

Ⅰ-13. 糖尿病病人的择医指导 ………………………………（ 63 ）
　　　Instructions on Treatment Selection for a Diabetic Patient

Ⅰ-14. 糖尿病病人的饮食指导 ………………………………（ 69 ）
　　　Dietary Instructions for a Patient with Diabetes Mellitus

Ⅰ-15. 癌症病人化疗前的护理 ………………………………（ 72 ）
　　　Nursing Care for a Cancer Patient before Chemotherapy

第二部分　外科护患沟通
Part Ⅱ　Surgical Nursing Care

Ⅱ-1. 颈椎骨折术后复健 ……………………………………（ 79 ）
　　　Post-operative Rehabilitation for a Patient with Fractured Cervical Spine

Ⅱ-2. 肌无力病人在气管切开前的恐惧 ……………………（ 84 ）
　　　A Myasthenia Patient's Fear before Tracheotomy

II-3. 高位截瘫病人的整体护理 ……………………… (88)
　　　Holistic Nursing Care for a High-level Paraplegia Patient
II-4. 多发性骨膜瘤病人的护理 ……………………… (93)
　　　Nursing Care for a Patient with Multiple Periosteoma
II-5. 车祸后病人的康复指导 ………………………… (96)
　　　Rehabilitation Instructions for a Patient in a Traffic Accident
II-6. 病人脊柱手术前的要求 ………………………… (100)
　　　A Patient's Request before a Spinal Surgery
II-7. 术中关爱 ………………………………………… (104)
　　　Caring in the Operating Room
II-8. 乳房纤维瘤术前焦虑的疏导 …………………… (107)
　　　Preoperative Guidance for an Anxious Patient with Breast Fibrosarcoma
II-9. 胃部术后舒适护理 ……………………………… (111)
　　　Comforting a Patient after a Gastric Operation
II-10. 乳房术前担忧疏导 ……………………………… (115)
　　　Counseling for an Anxious Patient before Breast Surgery
II-11. 产妇入院指导 …………………………………… (119)
　　　Admission Instructions for a Woman in Labor
II-12. 母乳喂养指导 …………………………………… (126)
　　　Guidance on Breast Feeding
II-13. 视网膜脱离病人的术前指导 …………………… (134)
　　　Preoperative Instructions for a Patient with Retinal Detachment
II-14. 巨大脑膜瘤术后饮食指导 ……………………… (138)
　　　Dietary Instructions after a Large Meningioma Surgery

Ⅱ-15. 心脏移植病人的心理护理 ……………………（143）
　　　Psychological Nursing Care for a Heart Transplant Patient

Ⅱ-16. 肾移植病人的全程护理 ……………………（150）
　　　Total Nursing Care for a Patient with Kidney Transplantation

Ⅱ-17. 冠脉搭桥术后病人便秘的护理指导 ……………（156）
　　　Post-operative Nursing Instructions on Constipation for a Coronary Artery Bypass Graft（CABG）Patient

第三部分　特殊人群（情境）沟通
Part Ⅲ　Nursing Care for Special Patient Groups

一、老年护理 …………………………………………（163）
Nursing Care for Senior Patients

Ⅲ-1. 老年人跌倒的防护 …………………………………（163）
　　　Preventing the Elderly from Falling Accidents

Ⅲ-2. 老年人的饮食指导 …………………………………（168）
　　　Dietary Instructions for the Elderly

Ⅲ-3. 老年性痴呆的护理 …………………………………（172）
　　　Nursing Care for a Patient with Senile Dementia

二、小儿患者的护理 …………………………………（176）
Nursing Care for Pediatric Patients

Ⅲ-4. 喘息性肺炎患儿的护理 ……………………………（176）
　　　Nursing Care for a Child with Asthmatic Pneumonia

Ⅲ-5. 腹泻患儿的护理 ……………………………………（180）
　　　Nursing Care for a Child with Diarrhea
Ⅲ-6. 肺炎患儿的护理 ……………………………………（184）
　　　Nursing Care for a Child with Pneumonia

三、感染病患者的护理 ……………………………（188）
Nursing Care for Patients with Infectious Diseases

Ⅲ-7. 人工肝治疗病人的术前宣教 ………………………（188）
　　　Pre-procedure Instructions for a Patient with Artificial Liver Treatment
Ⅲ-8. 重症肝炎病人的意识评估 …………………………（193）
　　　Evaluating the Level of Consciousness for a Patient with Severe Hepatitis
Ⅲ-9. 肝炎病人的休息指导 ………………………………（199）
　　　Instructions on Resting for a Hepatitis Patient

四、精神或心理问题的护理 ………………………（204）
Nursing Care for Patients with Psychiatric or Mental Problems

Ⅲ-10. 焦虑症病人的护理 …………………………………（204）
　　　 Nursing Care for a Patient with Anxiety Neurosis
Ⅲ-11. 神经性厌食病人的护理 ……………………………（207）
　　　 Nursing Care for a Patient with Anorexia Nervosa
Ⅲ-12. 疼痛用药的心理护理 ………………………………（211）
　　　 Psychological Nursing Care for a Patient Suffering from Pain

Ⅲ-13. 病人伤口愈合问题的心理护理 ································ （214）
　　　Psychological Nursing Care for a Patient with a Wound Healing Problem

五、家庭、社会或文化有关问题的护理 ····················· （219）
Nursing Care for Patients with Family, Social or Culture Related Problems

Ⅲ-14. 关切自我形象 ·· （219）
　　　Concerning Self-image

Ⅲ-15. 社交障碍病人的护理 ·· （223）
　　　Nursing Care for a Patient with Impaired Social Interaction

Ⅲ-16. 悲哀疏导 ·· （226）
　　　Counseling on Grieving

六、临床带教 ··· （229）
Clinical Nursing Instruction

Ⅲ-17. 整装待发实习 ··· （229）
　　　Getting Ready for Nursing Practicum

Ⅲ-18. 测量体温示教 ··· （232）
　　　Demonstration of Body Temperature Measuring Technique

附录　安宁照护 ··· （236）
Appendix　Hospice Care

第一部分 内科护患沟通
Part I Medical Nursing Care

第一部分　内科护患沟通

急诊 PTCA 病人的术前指导
Pre-procedure Instructions for an Emergency Percutaneous Transluminal Coronary Angioplasty（PTCA）Patient

杨小芳　陆敏霞

背景/ *Background*

王先生,52 岁,大学文化程度,因胸闷不适、胸痛 6 小时,ECG 示:"急性前壁心肌梗死"而入院。入院后医生决定为王先生立即行急诊 PTCA 术。王先生知道后,原本就十分紧张的他变得沉默起来。细心的床位护士小李发现了王先生的情绪变化,来到了病人床边。

Patient Mr. Wang, 52 years old with a college education, was hospitalized because of chest discomfort and pain for six hours. He was diagnosed by ECG to have an acute anterior myocardial infarction. The physicians decided to perform an emergency PTCA for him. When the very nervous Mr. Wang heard about this, he became very withdrawn. His nurse, Miss Li, perceived the change of his mood and went to talk to him.

Part I Medical Nursing Care

交流 / *Interactions*

护士：王先生,您胸痛好些了吗?

Nurse: Mr. Wang, is your chest pain getting better?

病人：唉!(王先生叹了口气)挂了这瓶水,胸痛已好多了。但是,刚才医生告诉我,要马上给我做手术,毕竟这是在心脏动手术,风险一定很大。我担心万一手术失败,我是否还能回到自己家?

Patient: (sighing) I feel much better now since they gave me the transfusion. But the doctor told me that I would need a surgery immediately. There are certain risks of having heart operations. Therefore, I am worried if I'll ever be able to go back home if the operation fails.

护士：是的,我非常能理解您现在的担忧。这个手术是有一定的风险,但是,我要告诉您,其实这是一种创伤很小的手术治疗方法,比外科手术风险小多了。手术时只需在您的大腿根部打上麻醉药,然后穿刺插管,就像平时打针一样稍微有些疼痛。我相信您一定能行,而且您在整个手术过程中始终是清醒的。

Nurse: Yes, I understand your concern very much. This procedure has some risk, but I should tell you that this procedure has much less risk when compared with the surgery because the incision is relatively very small. In this procedure, the physician will insert a tube into the femoral artery after local anesthesia. You will feel very little pain, almost like having an ordinary injection. Also during the procedure, you will be fully conscious. I am sure you can handle it.

病人：这些疼痛我倒是不怕,只是我的血管已经堵塞,怎么可能再打通呢? 万一不小心把血管捅破了,我不就没命了吗?

Patient: I am not afraid of the pain. But since my coronary artery is occluded completely, how can it be reopened? I will die if the blood vessel ruptures.

护士：您放心,我们几乎每个星期都有这种手术,还未发生过类似情况。况且,给您做手术的医生是一位非常有经验的主任。您瞧隔壁

第一部分　内科护患沟通

床的张大爷,都 74 岁了,上个星期也做了与您同样的手术,现在已下床活动啦。

Nurse: Don't worry. We perform this kind of operation almost every week without any incident. The doctor who will perform the procedure for you is a very experienced physician. The patient next to your bed, Mr. Zhang, 74 years old, underwent the same operation last week. He has recovered nicely and is out of bed moving around.

病人:哦,听你这么一说,我放心多了。

Patient: Really? This makes me feel much better now.

护士:为了让您术中、术后与医生更好地配合,我来给您简单讲一下手术过程及术后需注意的事项,好吗?

Nurse: OK. Now let me tell you a little bit about the procedure so that you'll be able to cooperate better with the medical personnel during and after the procedure. OK?

病人:太好啦,我的确很想知道这些内容。

Patient: That's great. I do want to know it.

护士:(拿出手中的宣教图片)您看这幅图,您的一根冠状动脉已被堵塞,导致一部分心肌长时间因缺血缺氧而坏死。手术时,医生首先在大腿根部的股动脉处穿刺,将导管送至冠状动脉口,注入造影剂,以明确病变的部位和程度。再根据造影结果,送入球囊导管,加压扩张球囊后,使堵塞的冠状动脉重新开通,恢复血流,必要时还将植入一枚金属支架,使冠状动脉持续扩张,就像图中的一样。我这样讲解,能让您理解吗?

Nurse: (taking out an illustration for the patient) Look at this picture, Mr. Wang. One of your coronary arteries is occluded. This has caused myocardial infarction due to lack of blood and oxygen to the myocardium for an extended period. So first, the physician will puncture the femoral artery and insert a catheter into the opening of the coronary artery. He will then take a coronary angiogram to determine where the stenosis is and its severity. Finally he will deliver a balloon catheter to dilate and reo-

Part Ⅰ　Medical Nursing Care

pen the occluded artery to allow the blood to flow. A stint will be planted if necessary. Do you understand my explanation?

病人：明白了。手术后我的心肌重新恢复了血液供应,我就不会有胸痛了,是吗?

Patient：Yes, I see. Therefore, I will have no more chest pain after the operation because of the re-supply of blood to the myocardium. Is this right?

护士：是的,一般情况下不会再发生胸痛。由于术中穿刺大动脉,为了避免伤口出血,术后您还需要平卧位休息24小时,动手术的那条腿要禁动12小时。如果无异常,24小时后您就可以适当在床上活动啦。

Nurse：Yes, usually there will be no more chest pain. However, because of the punctured femoral artery, you must stay in bed for 24 hours, and keep your leg from moving for 12 hours to avoid bleeding. You may move around in bed after 24 hours if nothing is wrong.

病人：是吗? 24小时不动,如果要小便,怎么办呢?

Patient：Really? Twenty-four hours? What should I do if I want to urinate?

护士：所以,现在开始,您就要在床上训练躺着排尿和进食。

Nurse：You must learn to urinate with a bed pan and eat in bed.

病人：好的,我会练的。

Patient：OK, I will.

结果 / Result

由于小李的耐心疏导和细心讲解,王先生消除了顾虑,以较好的心理状态接受了急诊PTCA手术治疗。术后24小时床上进食、排尿,局部穿刺伤口愈合良好。王先生高兴地称赞小李的一番术前谈话,对他来说真是非常有帮助的。

After Nurse Li's support and detailed explanation, Mr. Wang's worries were alleviated and he underwent the emergency PTCA at ease. He

第一部分　内科护患沟通

ate and urinated in bed within the first 24 hours after the procedure, and his local puncture site healed well. Mr. Wang was very happy, and praised Nurse Li for her pre-procedure talk. It was very helpful to him.

点评 / Comments

　　需进行急诊手术的病人，通常会出现不同程度的紧张、恐惧或担忧。护士小李巧妙地运用了移情、举例、阐明、讲解等方法，帮助病人消除了顾虑，顺利地接受了手术。

　　Patients who need an emergency operation usually have some levels of nervousness, fear, and anxiety. Nurse Li uses the methods of empathy, example, and explanation to alleviate the patient's worries, which helped him to face his operation.

Part I Medical Nursing Care

高血压病人的用药安全指导
Medication Safety Instructions for a Patient with Hypertension

沈琴　顾兰

背景 / Background

病人离休老干部徐某,78岁,因高血压、脑萎缩住院治疗。根据医嘱,需要补液。徐老常常在护士调节好补液滴速后自行加快滴速,使液体能在短时间内输完。床位护士发现后感到问题很严重,于是她与病人进行沟通。

Patient Mr. Xu, a 78-year-old retired official, was admitted to the hospital because of hypertension and brain atrophy. The doctor ordered fluid transfusion for him. However Mr. Xu wanted to finish the transfusion faster so he often increased the drip rate, which was set by the nurse. The nurse in charge discovered this and thought this was a very serious problem. She went to talk to him.

交流 / Interactions

护士: (边调节补液边说)徐老,滴速太快了,有什么不舒服吗?

第一部分　内科护患沟通

Nurse：(adjusting the rate of the IV drips) Good morning, Mr. Xu. Do you feel any discomfort because the drip rate is too fast?

病人：我现在感觉挺好的，没什么不舒服。

Patient：No, I am fine.

护士：您看，您现在的滴速是80滴/分，我想您是想快一点把补液滴完，是吗？

Nurse：Mr. Xu, you see, the rate of intravenous drips is 80 drops/min now. I think you just want to finish the transfusion sooner. Am I right?

病人：是的，我的心脏没什么问题，所以我把补液调快了。况且快点滴完后，还可以散散步，多活动活动。

Patient：Yes, there is no problem with my heart function. So I increased the rate. I would like to finish the transfusion sooner so I can take a walk and do some exercise.

护士：我很赞赏您这种活跃的心态。是的，适当的活动对老年人来说非常有益，但是，随着年龄的增长，身体内各脏器的功能也会随之减弱。比如说心脏，快速的输液会使大量的液体在短时间内积聚在心脏，加重心脏负担，从而引起许多的不适症状。轻者会引起胸闷、心跳加快，严重的会引起心功能衰竭。

Nurse：I admire your energetic attitude. It's true that proper exercise is very beneficial to older people. But the functions of organs will decrease with aging. Rapid transfusion will lead to the accumulation of fluid in the heart, increase the burden to the heart, and cause many uncomfortable syndromes, such as dyspnoea, rapid heart rate and even heart failure.

病人：你的话，我觉得很有道理。但是，我没有感到不舒服呀。

Patient：I think what you said is very reasonable. But I don't feel any discomfort at all.

护士：可能你自己感觉不到，但并不是说心脏没有加重负担。试想一下，如果有一架机器，你一直让它超负荷运转，机器会怎样呢？本

Part I Medical Nursing Care

来输液是为了营养脑细胞,但是如果因为输液过快引起心衰,那该多不划算呀?

Nurse: Maybe you can't feel that. But it doesn't mean the burden on the heart is not increased. Just think what will happen to a machine when it overworks? The original purpose of the transfusion is to give your brain cells more nutrition. Do you think it is worthwhile to risk potential heart failure to finish the transfusion a little faster?

病人:(笑了)好吧,小家伙,就听你的话,我不再调快滴速了。

Patient: (smiling) All right, young lady, I will follow your instructions and not increase the drip rate anymore.

护士:太好了,谢谢您的合作。我会尽量早一点为您补液,以便您有更多的活动时间,好吗?

Nurse: Great. Thank you for your cooperation. I will begin your transfusion as soon as possible so you can have more time to do other activities.

病人:好的,谢谢!

Patient: Good! Thank you.

结果 / Result

在责任护士的认真劝说下,徐老愉快地接受了建议,不再随意调节滴速。3周后,徐老病情好转,顺利出院。

Mr. Xu accepted the nurse's advice happily and didn't adjust the transfusion rate by himself anymore. He recovered well and was discharged 3 weeks later.

点评 / Comments

用药安全不仅是护理工作中重要的一部分,而且更关系到病人的治疗与护理效果,甚至生命安全。作为一名护士,应该常与病人沟

第一部分　内科护患沟通

通，做好病人用药方面的健康教育，告知病人忽视用药安全的危害性，提高病人的自护能力。

　　Medication safety is one of the most important parts in nursing. It influences the results of treatment and nursing care, and even the safety of the patient's life. Nurses should communicate with the patient often, provide health education on how to properly use the medication, its potentially harmful effects if one neglects safety, and improve the patient's ability to care for himself.

Part I   Medical Nursing Care

"先心"病人食道超声心动图检查前的指导
Instructions for a Patient with Congenital Cardiovascular Disease before a Transesophageal Echocardiogram

徐苏丹

患先天性心脏病房间隔缺损的方小姐,1小时以后将接受食道超声心动图检查,以明确病变程度,决定施行房缺封堵介入治疗。由于方小姐以前一直不知道自己患有先天性心脏病,这突如其来的打击,加上食道超声本身也是一个有创性检查,接下来又要做封堵手术,在短短的几天中,接二连三的刺激使方小姐感到十分焦虑和痛苦。尤其是想到一根粗粗的管子将要插入自己的食道,她感觉非常恐惧。这时,护士正在为方小姐做心理护理。

Miss Fang, who has been diagnosed with a congenital atrial septal defect, will receive a transesophageal echocardiogram in one hour to determine the degree of pathologic changes and to determine the use of the atrial septal defect occlusion treatment. Because Miss Fang was not previously aware of her illness, the diagnosis was a shock to her. Furthermore, the transesophageal echocardiogram was an invasive procedure after which she

第一部分　内科护患沟通

would also need to undergo an atrial septal defect occlusion treatment. All of these surprises in the last few days were worrying her tremendously. In particular, imagining a thick tube inserted into her esophagus really frightened her. The nurse was then giving Miss Fang psychological supportive care.

交流 / *Interactions*

护士：方小姐,看起来你脸色不太好,先坐一会儿,好吗?是不是有点紧张?

Nurse: Hello, Miss Fang. You look a little pale. Please sit down for a little while, OK? Are you a little nervous?

病人：是的,我非常紧张。做食道超声是不是很难受?时间会不会很长?我能受得了吗?

Patient: Yes, I am very nervous. Is the transesophagus echocardiograpy a very uncomfortable procedure? Does it take very long? Will I be able to handle it?

护士：检查前我们会给你用一些麻醉药的,这会让你感觉不是非常难受。当管子插入食道,只是在咽喉部时,你会感觉有点不舒服,可能会引起恶心反应。这时,你只要做吞咽动作,那样,医生插管就会很顺利。管子插入以后就不会再有什么刺激了,你也就不会太难受了。整个检查过程大约需要10分钟左右,我相信你一定可以坚持下来的。在检查过程中,你可以做深呼吸,来放松身体、减少紧张。

Nurse: We'll give you anesthesia prior to the test. So you won't feel too uncomfortable. When the tube is inserted into the esophagus, you will feel some discomfort. As it reaches the throat, it may make you feel nauseous. At this point, when that happens, try to swallow, which will allow the doctor to insert the tube smoothly. Once the tube is inserted, there won't be more irritation and you won't feel too much discomfort. The whole procedure takes about 10 minutes. I trust you can do it. During the procedure, it will help if you can take deep breaths to relax and reduce tension.

病人：有用吗?怎么做?

Part I Medical Nursing Care

Patient: Really? How?

护士:很多人这么做了都是有用的。检查时,你侧卧,双下肢自然弯曲,用腹部呼吸,深而慢,这样的呼吸会帮助你减少恶心反应。来,现在请你跟着我的提示做一遍试试,好吗?

Nurse: A lot of people find it helpful during the test to lie on your side, let your legs bend naturally, take deep and slow abdominal respiration. This will help to reduce the feeling of nausea. Here, you can follow my demonstration and give it a try.

病人:好。(几次深呼吸动作以后)我好像不像刚才那样心慌得厉害了。嗯……等会儿检查时,我可以让我母亲陪在我身边吗?

Patient: All right! (after several deep breaths) I no longer feel as flustered. Well, can my mom stay with me during the procedure?

护士:如果你真的需要母亲陪在身边,当然可以。不过,整个过程中我会一直陪在你身边,及时提醒你做深呼吸放松身体,配合医生检查。由我们一起来完成,好吗?

Nurse: If you really need her, she certainly can. However, I'll be by your side during the entire procedure to help you relax and cooperate with the doctor. We'll do it together. Is that all right?

病人:这样我就放心了。那就叫我母亲在外面等着吧,免得她也紧张。

Patient: This makes me feel much better. Then just let my mom wait outside. She won't be nervous this way.

护士:你真是个好女儿。

Nurse: You are such a good daughter.

病人:谢谢您。

Patient: Thank you!

结果 / Result

方小姐按照护士指导的方法主动配合,10分钟后顺利地完成了检查。结束时方小姐对护士说:"谢谢您一直陪着我,护士小姐,您教我的方法真管用,这项检查比我想象得要轻松一点。"

第一部分　内科护患沟通

Miss Fang actively cooperated with the process by following the nurse's advice. The procedure was successfully completed in 10 minutes. After the procedure, Miss Fang said to the nurse, "Thank you for staying with me the whole time. Your advice was very helpful. The test was easier than I thought."

点评 / *Comments*

检查前,经过护士切实有效的心理护理和详细的检查指导,病人方小姐解除了畏惧心理。在建立良好的医患关系的基础上,最大限度地调动了病人的自我调适能力。通过行为主义治疗方法,辅导病人进行放松训练,使方小姐检查前的紧张情绪得到了缓解,并顺利完成了检查。针对方小姐的恐惧、紧张心理,护士没有简单地劝其不要紧张,而是认同并接纳了方小姐紧张的情绪,表示出极大的理解。这种理解使病人对护士的信任瞬间被建立,使患者感觉到有人在帮她共同渡过生命中的一段艰难时期。

Prior to the test, the nurse's effective psychological support and detailed instructions helped to diminish Miss Fang's fear. The nurse was able to build a good relationship with the patient, and in turn greatly increased the patient's ability to adapt. By using Behavioral Therapy and teaching the patient how to relax, the nurse reduced Miss Fang's anxiety which finally contributed to a successful procedure. To reduce the patient's fear and nervousness, the nurse did not simply tell her not to worry, instead, the nurse showed understanding of the patient's fears and sympathized with her. This understanding allowed the patient to develop a sense of trust on the nurse immediately and was a great comfort to her as she believed somebody was helping her through a difficult time in her life.

Part I   Medical Nursing Care

慢性心力衰竭病人的健康指导
Health Instructions for a Patient with Chronic Heart Failure

杨小芳   陆敏霞

背景/ Background

张先生,63岁,因"扩张型心肌病、心衰"在2年内住院5次。由于疾病反复发作,经常住院,张先生觉得生活没有了希望,经常唉声叹气,愁眉不展。床位护士来到张先生床边,开始了他们的谈话。
Mr. Zhang, 63 years old, had been hospitalized five times in the last two years due to dilated cardiomyopathy and heart failure. Because of the reoccurrence of his illness and frequent hospitalization, Mr. Zhang felt that there was no hope in life and was often depressed. His nurse came to his bedside, and started a conversation.

交流/ Interactions

护士:老张,我看您这两天总是闷闷不乐,有什么心事吗?
Nurse: Mr. Zhang, you've looked unhappy the past couple of days. What's on your mind?

病人:唉!我年纪大了,心脏又不好,一年要住好多次医院,活着

第一部分　内科护患沟通

还有什么意思？

Patient: I am old and because my heart is not good, I have to be hospitalized several times a year. What's the point of living?

护士：不要太担心！前几次不都过来了吗？现在您能回忆一下前几次住院是因为什么原因吗？

Nurse: Don't worry too much. You were able to fight it through in the past, right? Can you recall what caused you to be hospitalized the past few times?

病人：第一次住院是因为我自己停药才发病的。有两次和这次一样都是因为感冒，还有一次是太疲劳。

Patient: The first time was because I stopped the medicine on my own. Twice like this time were because I had a cold, and once was due to fatigue.

护士：其实像您所说的疲劳、感冒是心衰最常见的诱发因素。除此之外，吃得太咸、情绪激动等也会诱发心衰。因此，您在日常生活中应注意休息，避免过度劳累，要注意保暖，预防感冒。饮食宜清淡低盐，易消化，而且要少食多餐，避免过饱。少吃含钠丰富的食物，如盐腌食物、碳酸饮料、罐头食品等，多吃蔬菜与水果，保持大便通畅。

Nurse: Actually cold and fatigue are the most common inducing factors for heart failure. Other than that, high salt intake and excitement can also induce heart failure. Because of that, you must have enough rest, avoid being too tired, and stay warm to prevent catching a cold. Your diet should have low salt and food that is easy to digest, also eat less in quantity but more frequently. Reduce your intake of sodium-rich foods such as pickled foods, carbonated beverages and canned goods. You should eat more fruit and vegetables to keep your bowel moving.

病人：我平时很喜欢吃咸鱼、咸菜，看来这些对我的心脏是有害的，而且我很贪凉，所以经常会感冒。如果我能照你说的去做，我就不会经常住院了，是吗？

Patient: I often like to eat salty fish and pickled vegetables. I see

Part I Medical Nursing Care

now these types of foods are not good for my heart. I also like the cooler temperatures and often catch a cold. If I follow your instructions, I will not be admitted to the hospital so often, right?

护士:是的,如果您能坚持的话,就可以减少住院次数。

Nurse: Yes, if you can stay persistent, you'll be able to reduce the frequency of hospitalization.

结果/ *Result*

在床位护士的耐心疏导与鼓励下,张先生重新鼓起了生活的勇气。住院2周后心功能得到了纠正,愉快地出院了。

Under the nurse's guidance and encouragement, Mr. Zhang regained his courage to live on. Two weeks later, his cardiac function was improved and he left the hospital cheerfully.

点评/ *Comments*

在对慢性心衰病人的护理过程中,由于疾病反复发作,病人往往会出现不同程度的情绪变化。护理人员应通过细致的观察及时发现病人的不良情绪,给予心理疏导,并做好健康宣教,既帮助病人增加了治病信心,又使病人获得了促进健康的知识。

Patients with chronic heart failure often have various degrees of mood swings due to the recurrence of their illness. Nursing staff should be aware of the patients' bad mood through careful observation and provide timely psychological support and health education. It will not only help the patients regain their confidence in the treatment, but also gain health related knowledge to promote their health.

第一部分 内科护患沟通

呼吸衰竭病人咳嗽排痰指导
Coughing and Expectoration Instructions for a Patient with Respiratory Failure

钮美娥 钱红英

背景 / Background

患者张某,男性,72岁,文盲,农民。因慢支急性发作而收住入院。入院后血气分析提示为"Ⅱ型呼衰"。入院时,床位护士发现该病人排痰不畅。护士小李来到床边进行护理。

Patient Mr. Zhang, a 72 year-old illiterate peasant, was hospitalized because of acute exacerbation of chronic bronchitis. The blood gas analysis after his admission indicated that he suffered type Ⅱ respiratory failure. The nurse understood the patient had a hard time coughing up his sputum during his admission. Nurse Li came to his bedside to provide nursing care.

交流 / Interactions

护士:你好,老张,今天感觉怎样?
Nurse: Hello, Mr. Zhang. How are you feeling today?

Part I Medical Nursing Care

病人：觉得喉咙口有痰，但就是咳不出。

Patient: I feel there is sputum in my throat but I cannot cough it up.

护士：你平时在家时每天喝多少水？

Nurse: How much water do you normally drink when you are at home?

病人：我不喜欢喝水，只有感到口渴时才喝。

Patient: I don't like to drink water, and only drink it when I feel very thirsty.

护士：哦，看来这样对你的排痰是很不利的。一般来讲，促进排痰有很多自我护理的方法，多喝水就是其中的一种。你每天最好能保证喝 1 200～1 500 毫升的水。

Nurse: Oh! That isn't good for sputum expectoration. There are many self-care strategies to promote sputum expectoration. Drinking water is one of these strategies. You should make sure to drink 1,200 to 1,500 mL of water every day.

病人：为什么要喝这么多水呀？

Patient: Why do I need to drink so much water?

护士：因为只有补充充足的水分，增加一定的体液量才可以稀释痰液，以助排痰。同时通过多饮水可增加排尿量，帮助排除体内废物。此外，多喝水还有利于预防感冒。

Nurse: Because sufficient water can dilute the sputum and make it easier to spit out. Drinking water can also increase the discharge of urine which contains metabolic wastes. Furthermore, it can also prevent the flu.

病人：原来喝水有这么多的好处，那我该怎么做才能完成这么多的饮水量？

Patient: Oh! It sounds like drinking more water is good for me. But how can I drink so much water?

第一部分　内科护患沟通

护士：你只要养成主动喝水的习惯，即不要等口渴以后再喝水，完成这点饮水量并不会太困难的。比如，你可以把喝水的时间安排在早晨起床后、三餐以后的 2 小时、睡前、夜间起床小便后。如果你待在空调房间的话，还可以适当增加饮水量，因为空调房间的空气比较干燥。

Nurse: It's not that difficult once you get in the habit of drinking water, which means drinking some water even when you don't feel thirsty. You can drink regularly, for example, right after you get up in the morning, 2 hours after your meals, before you go to sleep, and after urinating at night. Drink more when you are in an air-conditioned room where the air is usually drier.

病人：那除了多饮水之外，还有别的方法帮助排痰吗？

Patient: Are there other means to promote expectoration?

护士：有呀，现在我就可以教给你一种正确的咳嗽排痰的方法。

Nurse: Of course. Let me teach you how sputum can be spit out by coughing correctly.

（护士站在病人床边示范了正确的咳嗽排痰方法。）

(The nurse demonstrated to the patient.)

护士：好了，现在请你来做一遍吧。

Nurse: OK. Now try it yourself.

（病人在护士的指导下完成了正确的咳嗽排痰方法。）

(The patient tried it under the guidance of the nurse.)

护士：你做得不错，以后就可以这样做了。现在，我先去看其他病人了，过会儿再来给你做雾化吸入和捶背，你先休息吧。

Nurse: Well done. Keep doing this from now on. Now, have some rest. I am going to visit other patients and will be back to help you with mobilization therapy and to pat your back.

病人：好的，谢谢你。

Patient: Good, thank you.

Part I   Medical Nursing Care

点评/ Comments

在给病人作健康教育时,不但需要教会他方法,还应教会他执行措施的机理,这样病人才能自觉执行。

When carrying out health education to patients, the nurse should not only tell them what to do, but why, which will help the patients accept the advice more willingly.

第一部分　内科护患沟通

"肺心"病人安全用氧的指导
Oxygen Safety Instructions for a Patient with Chronic Pulmonary Heart Disease

钮美娥　钱红英

背景/ Background

患者赵某,男性,71 岁,小学文化,退休工人。反复咳、痰、喘30 余年。两周来胸闷、气急情况加重,门诊以"慢性肺源性心脏病"而收住入院。入院后血气分析提示"缺氧伴二氧化碳潴留",即给予止咳、化痰、平喘、抗炎等治疗,并给予控制性氧疗。

Patient Mr. Zhao is a 71-year old retired factory worker with an elementary school education. He has had repeated coughing, expectoration, and asthma for about 30 years. For the last two weeks he had been suffering worsening dyspnea and shortness of breath. He was admitted to the hospital and was diagnosed as having "chronic pulmonary heart disease". After admission, his blood gas analysis showed that he was suffering from hypoxemia and retention of carbon dioxide. He was given medication to treat the coughing, dilute the sputum, control the asthma, and control the inflammation. Controlled oxygen therapy was also carried out for him.

Part I　Medical Nursing Care

交流 / *Interactions*

护士：（带着准备齐全的吸氧用物来到床边）赵大伯，你好，你现在感觉胸闷，我给你吸点氧气，这个治疗会让你舒服一些的。

Nurse:（bringing all the things needed to the bedside for oxygen therapy）Hi, Mr. Zhao, I'll give you some oxygen since you are feeling distressed. This will make you feel more comfortable.

病人：好的。

Patient: OK.

护士：（非常熟练地完成了吸氧治疗系统）赵大伯，氧气给你接上了，你感觉如何？

Nurse:（skillfully setting up the oxygen inhalation therapy system）Mr. Zhao, I have connected the oxygen system for you. How are you feeling now?

病人：（看了一眼流量表）我现在气都接不上来，你怎么就给我开一点点氧气？

Patient:（looking at the flow meter of the oxygen tank）I feel short of breath. Why do you give me so little oxygen?

护士：哦，赵大伯，你误会了。根据你的病情，你需要低流量吸氧，我已经给你调节好流量了，你可不能自行调节哦。你先休息，过会儿我再来看你。

Nurse: Oh, Mr. Zhao, you do not understand. According to your present condition, you must be given the oxygen in a low flow level. I have adjusted the flow rate for you. You shouldn't change it by yourself. Please rest. I'll see you after a while.

（1小时后，护士来到床边，发现赵大伯面色潮红，多语，氧气流量已被调至8升/分。）

（One hour later, when the nurse came back, she found that Mr. Zhao had a red face, talking a lot, and the oxygen flow had been adjusted to 8 liters per minute.）

第一部分　内科护患沟通

护士：赵大伯,你怎么啦?（护士随手把氧流量调至原来的刻度。）

Nurse: Mr. Zhao, what's the matter with you? Are you OK? (The nurse adjusted the oxygen flow to the previous rate.)

病人：我怎么感觉比刚才更糟糕了?

Patient: Why am I feeling worse than before?

护士：你的氧气可不能调高呀。因为你目前的呼吸主要通过缺氧来反射刺激的,如果短时间内吸入过多氧气,虽然缺氧得到短暂改善,但这种反射刺激也随之减弱或消失,结果导致呼吸受到抑制,二氧化碳潴留会更加重。我现在给你施行的就是控制性氧疗,这样既可避免呼吸抑制,又可纠正你的缺氧和二氧化碳潴留。我这样解释你理解吗?

Nurse: You shouldn't have increased the oxygen flow by yourself. Because your breathing is stimulated by the reflex of hypoxia. If you inhale excessive oxygen in a short period of time, hypoxia might be improved transiently, but retention of carbon dioxide will get worse. What we are doing now is called controlled oxygen therapy which can prevent respiratory suppression, correct hypoxia and carbon dioxide retention. Do you understand my explanation?

病人：哦,原来是这样,我懂了。我再也不会自行调节流量了。

Patient: Yes, I see. I'll not adjust the oxygen by myself again.

点评 / Comments

在给病人实施任何护理措施时,都应该把所实施措施的目的、理论依据告知病人,使其正确理解。这样方能得到病人的主动配合,避免不良结果的发生。

When implementing a nursing intervention, it is necessary to tell the patient the purpose and reasons behind the intervention to obtain active cooperation from the patient and to avoid unexpected results.

Part I　Medical Nursing Care

咯血病人的健康宣教
Health Education for a Patient with Hemoptysis

钱红英　钮美娥

背景/ Background

患者赵某,男性,59岁,小学文化,退休工人。反复发作性慢性咳嗽伴脓痰3年,咯血1天,量约300毫升。平车入院,其妻子和儿子一起陪同在旁。入院诊断为"支气管扩张"。

Patient Mr. Zhao is a 59-year old retired factory worker with elementary school level education. He has had repeated chronic coughing with thick purulent sputum for three years and has spit about 300 milliliters of blood within the past day. He was brought to the hospital by ambulance, accompanied by his wife and son. His admission diagnosis was "bronchiectasis".

交流/ Interactions

护士:(床位护士小周面带微笑来到床边)你们好,我是床位护士,我姓周,你们就叫我小周吧。以后有什么事可以找我,我会尽我所能去做。你的床位医师姓张。

第一部分　内科护患沟通

Nurse:（His bed nurse, Miss Zhou, came to his bedside with a smile.）How do you do? I am your bed nurse. My last name is Zhou and Doctor Zhang is your doctor. Please call me any time if you need help.

病人:好的,谢谢你的介绍,麻烦你了。(说着,病人又一阵咳嗽,并咯出5口鲜血。患者及家属均表现出十分紧张的神色。)

Patient: OK, thank you. (Suddenly coughing, spitting out five mouthfuls of scarlet-colored blood, the patient and his family members became very nervous.)

护士:(在安置好病人后)现在舒服点了吧,你先安静地躺着,注意一定让自己身心放松,不要紧张。因为情绪紧张后会使自主神经的张力增加而导致喉肌痉挛,致使呼吸道变窄,气道内的血块不易咳出而影响呼吸,甚至会导致窒息,从而产生更严重的后果。

Nurse:（after taking care of the patient）Do you feel better now? You should lie in bed quietly, and try to relax and don't be too nervous. Emotional stress may increase the tension of the vagus nerve, resulting in a spasm of the laryngeal muscle which narrows the respiratory tracts. The blood clot in the airway will be difficult to remove by coughing. This might result in suffocation and produce more serious consequences.

病人:(表现出疑惑的神情)哦。

Patient:（with a suspicious expression）Oh.

护士:因为你现在还处在疾病的急性期,并且咯血量较大,所以你需要绝对卧床休息,尽量少说话,少活动。还有些注意事项你先听我讲,如有疑问可轻轻地问我。好吗?

Nurse: You are now in the acute stage of the disease. Because the amount of blood you spit out is large, you should lie in bed and don't talk or move too much. I'll tell you if there's something you should pay attention to. If you have any questions, you can ask me. OK?

病人:(微微点头,表示默许)

Patient:（nodded slightly）

护士:首先咯血病人的咳嗽一定要轻轻地,不能像你刚才那样。

Part I Medical Nursing Care

因为用力咳嗽会导致胸腔内压力增高而加重出血。其他可导致压力增高的因素还有用力屏气、用力大便等。所以你要尽量避免,尤其是排便问题更应引起重视,因为一方面卧床休息导致肠蠕动减弱,另一方面,可能你还不能习惯于床上排便,所以很容易产生便秘。在通常情况下,可通过进食富含纤维素的食物,多饮水,避免食辛辣等刺激性食物,注意每天按摩腹部来保持大便通畅。

Nurse: First, a patient with hemoptysis must try to cough gently and shouldn't cough as you did a few moments ago. Coughing with too much force will lead to increased pressure of the thoracic cavity and aggravate bleeding. There are other factors that can increase the pressure of the thoracic cavity, such as holding your breath, defecating with force, etc. So you should try to avoid those behaviors. Attention should be paid especially to defecating, because lying in bed weakens the movements of one's intestines and most people are not accustomed to defecating in bed. People confined to bed are prone to have constipation. However, constipation can be avoided by eating food rich in fiber, drinking lots of water, avoiding spicy food, and performing stomach massages every day.

病人妻子:我们老赵平时喜欢进偏烫的食物,这对他的疾病有影响吗?

Patient's Wife: My husband likes eating very hot food. Will it affect his disease?

护士:这就是接下来我要跟你们说的话题。目前老赵宜进食温凉、清淡的流质或半流质食物。因为食物的温度偏高不利于止血。

Nurse: This is a topic that I want to discuss with you. At present, lukewarm, cool, light liquid or semi-liquid food is suitable for your husband. Hot food is not good for the prevention of bleeding.

病人妻子:谢谢你跟我们讲那么多。

Patient's Wife: Thank you for telling us so many things.

第一部分 内科护患沟通

点评/ Comments

当新病人刚入院时,切忌"满堂灌"。必须结合病人当时的情景,有所侧重地讲解目前病人最需要的知识点。

When a patient is newly admitted to the hospital, you should not give him/her too much information at once. You should first explain in detail the most necessary information according to the patient's conditions.

Part I　Medical Nursing Care

机械通气病人的健康指导
Health Instructions for a Patient with Mechanical Ventilation

钱红英　钮美娥

背景/ *Background*

患者王某,男性,61 岁,小学,退休工人。因反复胸闷、气喘 30 余年,病情加重 1 周入院。入院后查血气分析示 PaO₂ 45 mmHg, PaCO₂ 70 mmHg。入院后即给予补液、抗炎、平喘、吸氧等治疗。

A 61-year old male patient who is a retired factory worker with an elementary school level education has chest distress and a 30-year history of asthma. He was admitted to the hospital after 1 week of aggravated symptoms. His blood-gas analysis showed PaO_2 45 mmHg and $PaCO_2$ 70 mmHg. After admission, he was treated with fluid replacement, anti-inflammation, asthma control, and oxygen therapies.

交流/ *Interactions*

护士:老王,你已经吸了 2 个小时的氧气了,感觉如何?
Nurse: Mr. Wang, you have been under oxygen therapy for two hours now. How do you feel?

第一部分　内科护患沟通

病人：(较烦躁地摆摆手)不行,我还是觉得闷,透不过气来。我总感觉呼吸时特别累。

Patient: (waving his hands impatiently) Not so good. I still feel distressed. I am having a hard time breathing. I just feel so exhausted.

护士：我知道了。你试试先休息一会儿,我马上去向医生汇报。

Nurse: I see. Try to rest for a moment. I'll call the doctor now.

(护士再次来到病人床边。)

(The nurse came back to the patient again.)

护士：老王,医生刚才来看过你了。我现在遵医嘱,准备给你使用无创呼吸机,让呼吸机来帮助你呼吸,这样你可能会感觉舒服点。

Nurse: Mr. Wang, the doctor has come by to check on you. Following his order, I am going to put you on a non-invasive breathing machine. It will help you breathe, so you can feel more comfortable.

病人：(很紧张地摇摇手)不要,不要,我不要上呼吸机。我等会儿就会好起来的。

Patient: (waving his hands nervously) No, no. I don't want to use the machine. I'll be better in a moment.

护士：(微微一笑)老王,你别紧张。这种呼吸机不是我们以前所用的呼吸机,这是一种小型的呼吸机,对你影响不大。使用时,我们会给你佩戴一个面罩,你所要做的只是跟平常一样呼吸就行了。

Nurse: (smiling) Mr. Wang, don't be so nervous. This isn't the same kind of respirator we used in the past. It is a mini-respirator, with few unfavorable effects. We will put a face mask on you, and all you need to do is to breathe normally.

病人：(很疑惑地)是吗?

Patient: (puzzled) Really?

护士：是的,你看,我已经把呼吸机带来了。

Nurse: Yes, you see, here is the respirator.

病人：(转过头看了一下)哦。

Patient: (turning his head to look at the machine) Oh.

Part I Medical Nursing Care

护士：老王,我现在把呼吸机的参数调好,把管道连接好以后给你把面罩带上好吗?

Nurse: Mr. Wang, let me adjust the parameters of the respirator and the tube connections first, then I will help you put on the mask. Is that all right?

病人：(无奈地)那就试试吧。

Patient: (reluctantly) OK. Let's have a try.

护士：(动作熟练地完成了操作)老王,固定带的松紧合适吗?

Nurse: (finishing the operation dexterously) Mr. Wang, are the straps of the mask on properly?

病人：(点点头)

Patient: (nodding his head)

护士：(帮助病人整理床单)

Nurse: (helping clean the patient's bed)

病人：(表情很痛苦,用手指着面罩)

Patient: (pointing to the face mask with a painful expression)

护士：(协助把面罩取下)怎么啦?

Nurse: (taking off the face mask) What's the matter?

病人：不行,不行,我觉得更闷了。我还是像刚才那样吸氧气吧。

Patient: It is not working. I feel even more distressed. I'd rather go back to the oxygen therapy.

护士：老王,刚开始上这种呼吸机时,好多病人会出现与你一样的情况。你只要坚持几分钟就会适应的。我们再来试一下,好吗?

Nurse: Mr. Wang, many patients have experienced the same feelings when they first put on the mask. If you endure for a few minutes, you will get used to it. Let's try it again, OK?

病人：(叹气)好吧。

Patient: (sighing) OK.

护士：(再次帮病人把面罩固定好,拍拍病人肩膀)老王,就跟平时

第一部分 内科护患沟通

一样呼吸好了,不要刻意屏气。对,就像现在这样,不错,我在这儿看着呢。

Nurse：(helping the patient put on the mask again, and patting his shoulder) Mr. Wang, breathe normally. Don't hold your breath. Right, that's it. Not bad. I will stay here to observe you.

病人：(点点头)

Patient：(nodding)

护士：(站在床边观察了5分钟)老王,现在感觉如何,是否比刚才好多了?

Nurse：(observing for about 5 minutes) Mr. Wang, how are you feeling now? Do you feel better?

病人：(点点头)

Patient：(nodding)

点评 / Comments

任何护理措施不是做完就了事。执行后的观察非常重要,也更有利于及时发现问题,解决问题,从而提高护理措施的效果。

Nursing care is not accomplished by just carrying out the procedures. It is important to follow up with close observation to help catch problems in time to solve them, and to enhance the effectiveness of the nursing interventions.

总点评 / Conclusions

奥瑞姆提出的自理模式中,强调了人的自理能力,提出护理活动是一种根据护理对象的自理需要、自理能力而设计的一系列帮助性服务。他认为当健康缺陷时,满足人自理需要的护理工作主要有帮助护理对象：①有效遵循诊断、治疗和康复措施;②认识并应付病理状态的影响和后果;③认识、应付和调整治疗措施带来的不适和不良反应;④修正自我概念和自我印象;⑤学会在病理状态下生活。

Part I Medical Nursing Care

Orem's self-care nursing model emphasizes the self-care abilities of the patients. This model points out that nursing activities are a series of assistant services designed in line with the self-care needs and self-care abilities of the patients. Orem thought that when the health of a person is defective, self-care nursing can help patients to: (1) effectively carry out the interventions including diagnostic, treatment, and rehabilitation, (2) understand and cope with the influences and outcomes of the diseases, (3) recognize and deal with malaise and side-effects of the therapies, (4) modify self-concept and self-image, and (5) live with diseases.

第一部分　内科护患沟通

消化性溃疡病人用药指导
Medication Instructions for a Patient with Peptic Ulcer

胡秀英

背景/ Background

　　病人李某,女,32岁,外企职员。因剑突下疼痛一周入院,既往有夜间痛史,胃镜检查结果:胃、十二指肠复合性溃疡。病人由于对疾病不了解,同时又担心工作问题,情绪焦虑,常对医务人员抱怨治疗效果不佳,对治愈疾病缺乏信心。此时床位护士小顾来到床边进行护理。

　　Patient Ms. Li is a 32-year-old foreign-owned corporation employee. She was admitted to the hospital because of epigastric pain for a week. She has a history of night pain. The gastroscopy examination indicated that she had a gastric-duodenum complex ulcer. Because she did not know much about the disease and was worried about her job, the patient was anxious and often complained to the medical staff that the treatment was not effective. She was not confident of her recovery. Miss Gu, the nurse in charge of her, went to care for her.

Part I Medical Nursing Care

交流 / Interactions

护士：李女士，您经过5天的治疗，现在觉得好一点了吗？

Nurse: Hello, Ms. Li. Are you feeling better after five days of treatment?

病人：好是好一点了，但我觉得治疗得太慢，是不是你们给我的药不对啊？

Patient: A little better. But I feel the results of the treatment are coming too slow. Have you been giving me the right medicine?

护士：李女士，现在我们给您使用的都是针对您疾病的制酸药、保护胃黏膜的药物。

Nurse: Ms. Li, the medications we've given you are for gastric acid control and to protect the gastric mucous membrane. They are appropriate for your illness.

病人：那为什么治疗得这么慢？

Patient: Why am I recovering so slowly?

护士：李女士，您所患的疾病是由于胃肠黏膜被消化液自身消化而造成的溃疡，是一种慢性病，需要坚持长期治疗后溃疡面才能慢慢修复愈合，疼痛才能完全缓解。现在才刚治疗5天，不可能这么快病就好了。

Nurse: Ms. Li, you are suffering from a peptic ulcer, which is caused by the digestion of the gastric mucous membrane by your own gastric acid. It's a chronic disease. Healing the ulcer and completely relieving the pain can only be achieved after lengthy treatment. You have only been treated for five days. It is not enough time to completely recover yet.

病人：可我已经住院5天了，公司又一大堆事情等着我去处理。你们再给我用些好药，让我尽快治好出院。

Patient: But I have stayed in the hospital for five days and there are so many things in my company waiting for me to handle. Please prescribe some better medicine for me so that I can be discharged sooner.

第一部分　内科护患沟通

护士：我们现在给您用的已经是好的了。您不要着急,情绪焦虑对疾病治疗恢复不利,反而会刺激胃酸分泌增加,加重病情。

Nurse: The medicine we are using are the best. Relax. Anxiety is not good for recovery. It stimulates the secretion of gastric acid and makes your illness even worse.

病人：照你这么说,我的病很难治好了?

Patient: According to what you have said, it's difficult to cure my illness?

护士：不是的,你不要对治疗这么没信心。我们病房现在正好住了一位和您患有同样疾病的先生,他经治疗后已基本痊愈,准备择日出院。等会儿我介绍他和你认识,你们可以交流一下治疗的情况,好吗?

Nurse: No, don't be so pessimistic. Currently there is a patient in our ward who has the same disease as you. He has almost recovered completely and is preparing for discharge. I will introduce him to you later, and you can talk to him about the treatment. Is that all right?

病人：好吧。他真的好了吗?

Patient: OK. Has he really recovered?

护士：是真的。你现在最主要的是放松心情,保持愉快良好的情绪。我这有一本《笑话全集》介绍给你看,希望对你有所帮助。我一会儿再来看你,有什么不舒服告诉我或者直接按铃招呼我好吗?

Nurse: Really. Now the most important thing for you to do is to relax and try to be cheerful. I have a comic book. I'll let you read it and hope it will help you relax. I'll come back to see you after a while. If you feel uncomfortable, please tell me or press the call button. OK?

病人：好的。

Patient: OK.

点评/ Comments

在对慢性疾病患者的护理过程中,最为重要的是要深切理解和同情患者的痛苦和不幸,体谅他们因病魔缠身而产生的不正常的情绪和

Part I   Medical Nursing Care

行为,同时又要使他们认识到坚持配合治疗的重要性。遇有言语不周对护理人员缺乏应有信任时,护理人员不能感情用事,要以理解和真诚来感化他们。就如顾护士那样,巧妙地应用解释说明、举例、转移注意力等方法,因势利导地转化矛盾。

When nursing care of patients with chronic illness, the most important thing is to understand and sympathize with the patients' pain and misfortune. We must be considerate about the patients' abnormal mood and behavior caused by the illness, and at the same time try to make them realize the importance of persistence and cooperation with the treatment. The more difficult and pessimistic the patient, the more consideration and sincerity we should display. The methods we may use, such as those Miss Gu applied, including explanation, illustration, and transferring attention, can help to minimize the conflict between the nurses and the patients.

第一部分　内科护患沟通

病毒性脑炎病人的护理援助
Nursing Support for a Patient with Viral Encephalitis

徐琴娟

背景/ *Background*

病人石英英,女性,45岁,病毒性脑炎。有一儿子,在饭店上班,丈夫长期出差在外。患者神志清楚。视物模糊,四肢活动佳。某日中午11点多,病房内患者都在吃中饭,而石英英半坐在床上望着窗外发呆。这时床位护士来到病床前。

Patient Shi Yingying is a 45-year-old female patient with viral encephalitis. She has a son who works at a restaurant, and her husband works out of town. She is conscious and mobile, but has blurred vision. One day, at about 11 am, all the other patients were having their lunch except Shi Yingying who was sitting on her bed and staring out the window. At this time the nurse in charge came to her bedside.

交流/ *Interactions*

护士: 石女士,你口渴吗？要喝水吗？（病人回过头来,笑笑。护

Part I　Medical Nursing Care

士把水杯端上,吸管送到口边,石英英喝着水。)

Nurse: Mrs. Shi, are you thirsty? Would you like to drink some water? (The patient turned and smiled at the nurse. The nurse gave a glass of water to her, and helped her with the straw. Mrs. Shi drank the water.)

护士:你怎么还不吃饭?儿子还没送过来吗?

Nurse: Why aren't you having lunch? Has your son brought your lunch yet?

病人:今天我儿子上早班,要下午三点钟才下班。昨天跟他讲好了,我自己随便买点吃的,等一会儿我去食堂买就好了。

Patient: No. He works the early shift today and will not finish work until 3 p.m. I told him yesterday that I would just buy something for lunch myself. I will go and get something from the dining room in a few minutes.

护士:哦,我一会儿就下班了,我来帮你买饭好了。

Nurse: Well, I can buy lunch for you after I finish my work.

病人:不要不要,太麻烦了,我自己去好了。

Patient: No, no. I don't want to trouble you too much. I'll do it myself.

护士:没关系的,你看东西不清楚,单独出去我也不太放心,若路上摔跤了,那可怎么办。我反正是顺便,好了,就这么说定了,我去交班,你等我噢!(11点40分,护士端着饭菜来到石英英床前。)

Nurse: It's OK. You can't see too well and I'll be worried if you go out alone. What if you fell down on the way? I'm going to give my off-duty report now. Just wait for me. (At 11:40, the nurse brought the lunch to Shi Yingying.)

护士:石女士,你需要多吃点富含维生素的食物。我买了番茄炒蛋、空心菜、清蒸鱼,希望你喜欢。(病人坐起身,感激地望着护士。)

Nurse: Mrs. Shi, you need food rich in vitamins. I bought you fried tomatoes with eggs, fresh vegetables and steamed fish. Do you like them? (The patient sat up and looked at the nurse gratefully.)

病人:喜欢,喜欢,真是太感谢你了。

Patient: They are all my favorites. Thank you very much.

护士:不用谢,下次碰到这种情况你尽管对我们说好了。其实,你还是订医院营养室的饭菜吧,这样就不用你儿子每餐都要记着来送饭。如果你觉得饭菜不合胃口,就对我说,让我来和营养室联系,为你另外配餐。好了,你慢慢吃吧。

Nurse: Don't mention it. Next time don't hesitate to tell us when you need help. By the way, I think it's better for you to reserve your meals from the hospital cafeteria, so you don't have to depend on your son to bring in your food. If the cafeteria meals are not to your taste, let me know. I'll contact the cafeteria to make a menu specifically for you. Now, enjoy your lunch.

结果/ Result

病人满意地用完了午餐,并且在护士的帮助下,在营养室预订了适合口味的饭菜。

The patient finished her lunch happily. With the help of the nurse she also reserved her favorite food from the hospital cafeteria.

点评/ Comments

助人为乐是一种高尚的道德品质,也是一种良好的心理素质,更是护理人员职业素质的重要组成部分,是在后天的学习、生活、工作、教育等实践活动过程中逐渐形成和发展起来的。作为一名优秀的护士,当想病人所想,急病人所急,痛病人所痛,以职业特有的温柔、细致、勤劳,尽力为护理对象解除困难和疾苦,这才无愧于"白衣天使"的光荣称号。

Part I Medical Nursing Care

Helping others is a noble quality as well as a good mental quality. It's an important ingredient of nursing professional ethics. It is acquired and gradually developed through the process of learning, living, working and education. To be an excellent nurse, we should care about the patients' thought, be concerned with patients' worries, and empathize with patients' pain. We should do our best to relieve the patients' suffering and difficulties with professional gentleness, carefulness and diligence. This is what "Angel in White" is all about.

第一部分　内科护患沟通

脑神经多普勒检查情景会话
Conversations during a Doppler Cerebral Ultrasonic Examination

惠品晶

11.1　偏头痛
Migraine

背景/ *Background*

病人王女士,30岁,因头痛、头晕2周而来院检查。

Patient Ms. Wang, 30 years old, came to the hospital to have an examination because she had headaches and dizziness for 2 weeks.

交流/ *Interactions*

检查者：你感觉有些累吧,先坐下休息片刻。

Examiner: Are you feeling tired? Please sit down and rest for a moment.

病人：这是什么检查?

Patient: What kind of examination is this?

检查者：是经颅超声多普勒。你有什么不舒服吗?

Examiner: It's a Transcranial Doppler Ultrasonogram (TCD). Are

Part I Medical Nursing Care

you not feeling well?

病人：我感到头晕、头痛。

Patient: I feel dizzy and have a headache.

检查者：以前有过这种头痛吗？

Examiner: Have you ever had this kind of headache before?

病人：是的，但没这么严重。

Patient: Yes, but not so severe.

检查者：以前做过什么检查吗？

Examiner: What kind of examination did you have before?

病人：CT 检查。

Patient: CT.

检查者：结果如何？

Examiner: What was the result of your CT examination?

病人：正常。

Patient: Normal.

检查者：请躺在检查床上，我给你检查一下。

Examiner: Please lie down on the bed. I will examine you right away.

病人：好的。

Patient: OK.

检查者：疼痛是间歇性还是持续性的？

Examiner: What kind of pain do you have? Is it intermittent or persistent?

病人：间歇性的。我是左侧头痛，你要检查这边。

Patient: Intermittent. The headache is in my left side and you should examine there.

检查者：你放心，环主干的血管都要检测。你现在起来，坐在这，检测椎基底动脉。

Examiner: Don't worry. The main brain vessels will be all examined. Please get up and sit down for the vertebrobasilar artery examination.

第一部分　内科护患沟通

病人：我有问题吗？

Patient: Do I have a problem?

检查者：是脑供血不足。

Examiner: The blood supplied to your brain is not sufficient.

病人：那我头痛是怎么回事？

Patient: What causes my headache?

检查者：这是脑血管痉挛所致的相对供血不足，是功能性的改变。

Examiner: The blood supply is relatively insufficient because of the cerebral vasospasm. It is the functional change of the blood vessels.

病人：我明白了。

Patient: I see.

检查者：这是你的检查报告，把它给你的医生看。

Examiner: Here's your report. Show this to your doctor.

11.2　椎基底动脉供血不足
Insufficient Blood Supply of the Basilar and Vertebral Arteries

背景 / Background

男性，56岁，近2天头晕，体位改变时明显。

A 56-year-old male patient felt dizziness especially while changing body positions in the last couple of days.

交流 / Interactions

检查者：你有什么不舒服？

Examiner: What kind of discomfort do you have?

病人：我头晕，体位改变时尤其明显。

Patient: I feel dizzy especially when changing body positions.

Part I Medical Nursing Care

检查者:这种情况有多久了?

Examiner: How long have you been like this?

病人:有两三天了。

Patient: Two or three days.

检查者:请躺在检查床上,我给你检查一下。

Examiner: Lie down on the bed please. I'll examine you.

病人:我的情况怎样?

Patient: What's my condition?

检查者:你的颈内动脉系检查正常。你慢慢起床,坐在这,我再检查椎基底动脉。

Examiner: Your internal carotid artery system is normal. Get up slowly and sit down please. Let me check your vertebrobasilar artery.

病人:哦,我现在正头晕呢。

Patient: Oh, I'm feeling dizzy now.

检查者:别紧张,让我扶你一下。

Examiner: Take it easy. Let me help you.

检查者:现在感觉好些了吗?

Examiner: Do you feel better now?

病人:好点儿了。

Patient: Yes. Thanks.

检查者:我要给你进行转颈试验。

Examiner: I will give you a neck rotation test.

病人:你看我该怎么办呢?

Patient: What should I do?

检查者:你放松,别紧张。

Examiner: Relax. Don't be nervous.

病人:我查的结果如何?

Patient: What's the result?

检查者:是椎动脉供血不足。

Examiner: It's the insufficiency of blood supply from the vertebral ar-

第一部分　内科护患沟通

tery（VA）。

病人：谢谢你。

Patient: Thank you.

检查者：不客气。去看医生,接受治疗,祝你早日康复。

Examiner: You are welcome. Please see a doctor for treatment. I hope you have a quick recovery.

点评/ *Comments*

颈部椎动脉起始部、颅内椎动脉近端和基底动脉近端动脉粥样硬化病变上新发生的血栓,这三处是后循环发生动脉粥样硬化最常见的部位。体位相关性椎动脉内血栓常在颈部处于特殊位置时发生。业已证实,如游泳、健身操、射箭及摔跤等易引发椎动脉内血栓。

Most thrombosis of atherosclerotic lesions occurs at the origin of the VAs in the neck, the proximal intracranial VAs, and the proximal basilar artery. Positional related thrombi in the VA may happen during periods of unusual neck posturing. It has been documented that thrombus is easy to form in vertebral artery when swimming, doing fitness exercises, practicing archery, and wrestling.

11.3　蛛网膜下腔出血
Subarachnoid Hemorrhage（SAH）

背景/ *Background*

患者男性,52 岁。5 天前突然剧烈头痛、呕吐,出现短暂性意识丧失,现在神志清楚。CT:蛛网膜下腔出血。DSA:右侧大脑中动脉瘤。

A 52-year-old male patient suddenly had severe headaches, vomiting, and transient unconsciousness 5 days ago. Currently, the patient regains consciousness. CT: Subarachnoid hemorrhage. DSA: Right MCA

Part I   Medical Nursing Care

aneurysm.

交流 / Interactions

检查者：你小心点儿，不要动，就在平车上检查。

Examiner: Be careful. Do not move. I will check you right away on the stretcher.

病人：为什么？

Patient: Why?

检查者：防止再出血。

Examiner: To avoid another hemorrhage.

病人：谢谢。

Patient: Thank you.

检查者：检查时你保持安静。你的头尽量保持不动。

Examiner: Keep quiet and don't move your head as long as you can during the examination.

病人：好的。

Patient: OK.

（检查完毕）

(after the examination)

病人：你发现什么了吗？

Patient: What have you found?

检查者：目前有脑血管痉挛。这是你的检查报告，给医生看。

Examiner: There is a vasospasm in your cerebral vessels. Here's your report. You should give it to your physician.

病人：多谢。

Patient: Thank you very much.

点评 / Comments

原发性蛛网膜下腔出血的早期特征性临床表现是突发剧烈头痛。其发病的急骤性和疼痛的剧烈程度非常引人注目。头痛常在数秒至1

第一部分　内科护患沟通

分钟内达到极严重程度,以致病人不得不改变活动形式。病人意识变化常常很快,包括可在数分钟内丧失意识。发病时常呕吐。蛛网膜下腔出血常是囊状动脉瘤破裂所致。这种动脉瘤有时可被 CT 或 MRI 发现,但为了证实这种病变,常需做能显示全部颅内血管的动脉造影。

The early clinical characteristic of primary SAH is the sudden onset of severe headache. The suddenness of the onset and the severity of the pain are usually dramatic. The headache commonly reaches a severe intensity in a matter of seconds to a minute and is so severe that the patient has to change the pattern of activity. Often there is a rapid alteration of level of consciousness including becoming unconscious in a few minutes. Vomiting at the onset is frequent. SAH is usually due to a rupture of saccular aneurysm. The aneurysm can sometimes be viewed on CT or MRI. But usually an arteriogram is needed to show all the intracranial vessels, and find the lesion.

11.4　颈动脉颅外段严重狭窄
Severe Stenosis in Extracranial Carotid Artery

背景/ Background

病患男性,68 岁,退休教师,吸烟史 30 余年,高血压史 10 余年。头晕、晕厥,右手握笔无力 2 天。

A 68-year-old male patient, who is a retired teacher, has a smoking history of over 30 years and hypertension for 10 years. He experienced dizziness, syncope and felt weak while holding his pen in his right hand for the last 2 days.

交流/ Interactions

检查者:你头痛吗?

Part I   Medical Nursing Care

Examiner: Do you have a headache?

病人:不痛,就是感到头晕。

Patient: No, I just feel dizzy.

检查者:你感到这样有多久了?

Examiner: How long have you been feeling like this?

病人:从前天开始突然发作的。

Patient: It all started the day before yesterday.

检查者:你高血压有多久了?

Examiner: How long have you suffered from hypertension?

病人:我知道有10年了。

Patient: About ten years as far as I know.

检查者:你家里还有人有这病吗?

Examiner: Are there any other members in your family suffering from the same disease?

病人:是的,我父亲有高血压。

Patient: Yes, my father has hypertension.

检查者:你吸烟吗?

Examiner: Do you smoke?

病人:是的。

Patient: Yes, I do.

检查者:我劝你不要吸烟了。

Examiner: My advice to you is to give up smoking.

病人:好的。我的检查结果如何?

Patient: OK. What's the result of the examination?

检查者:你的左侧颈内动脉颅外段狭窄。

Examiner: There is a stenosis at the left extracranial internal carotid artery.

病人:我的情况很严重吗?

Patient: Is my condition serious?

检查者:因为颅内侧支循环良好,所以你的临床症状不明显,但需

第一部分　内科护患沟通

要进一步检查。

Examiner: There's adequate intracranial collateral circulation. The symptom is not very clear. I suggest you have an additional examination to confirm the result.

病人:做哪些检查?

Patient: What kind of examination do you suggest?

检查者:DSA 或 MRA。

Examiner: A DSA or MRA.

检查者:这是你的检查报告,现在拿去给医生看。

Examiner: Here's your report. You should give it to your physician right away.

病人:多谢。

Patient: Thank you very much.

点评 / Comments

颈段颈内动脉闭塞不引起任何特征性的临床征候。在颅内有丰富的侧支循环时,颈内动脉闭塞可无症状体征,但也可引起短暂性脑缺血发作,甚至引起同侧半球重要部分的梗死。在颈内动脉闭塞或狭窄时,可因动脉至动脉的栓塞或阻塞血管的血凝块向远端扩延至大脑中动脉主干而引起脑梗死。

Occlusion of the internal carotid artery in the neck does not usually produce any characteristic clinical picture. In the presence of adequate intracranial collateral circulation, internal carotid artery occlusion may produce no signs or symptoms. But it might cause temporary tissue hypoxia, and it may result in anything from a TIA to infarction of a major portion of the ipsilateral hemisphere. Carotid occlusion or stenosis may also cause cerebral infarction by artery-to-artery embolism or by propagation of an occluding clot distally into the stem of the middle cerebral artery.

Part I Medical Nursing Care

11.5　短暂性脑缺血发作
Transient Cerebral Ischemic Attack

背景 / Background

患者66岁,教授,突发失语和右手无力。他的妻子和一位朋友将其送入医院。身体检查显示Broca's失语和右侧轻偏瘫。20小时内消退。

A 66-year-old professor suddenly developed aphasia and weakness in his right hand. His wife and a friend took him to the hospital. The physical examination indicated Broca's aphasia and right hemiparesis. Both were resolved within 20 hours.

交流 / Interactions

检查者:你感觉怎么样?

Examiner: How do you feel?

病人:我曾经不会说话,右手无力。

Patient: I could not speak and my right hand was weak.

检查者:那是什么时候?

Examiner: When did it happen?

病人:20小时前。

Patient: About twenty hours ago.

检查者:来,我扶你慢慢躺在检查床上。

Examiner: Let me help you lie down slowly on the examination bed.

病人:好的。这是什么检查?

Patient: OK. What is this examination?

第一部分 内科护患沟通

检查者：经颅多普勒超声。

Examiner: A Transcranial Doppler Ultrasonogram.

病人：它能检查哪些血管?

Patient: Which cerebral vessels can it detect?

检查者：哦,颅内大血管。

Examiner: The main intracranial cerebral arteries.

检查者：你打算干什么?

Examiner: What are you going to do?

病人：哦,我只想休息休息。

Patient: Oh, I just want to take a rest.

检查者：这是你的检查报告,现在拿去给医生看。

Examiner: Here's your report. You should give it to your physician right away.

病人：多谢。

Patient: Thank you very much.

点评 / Comments

由于病人的病情可不断发生变化,故必须说明有关检查的时间和症状发生的时间。因为观察时间不同,病人的病情也不同。发病时的特点,包括活动、如何起病、起病时的体位及功能发展到最严重程度的速度等均有助于判断卒中是否已发生,也有助于判断其类型。例如,有过短暂性脑缺血发作症状时,则梗死引起卒中的可能性比出血更大。发病时的意识改变、剧烈头痛或呕吐及发病后的体征演变都很重要,因其有助于判定卒中的类型、定位和预后。

Since the patient's status may be changing, it should be stated in relation to the time of assessment and the time of onset of the symptoms. At various times during observation, the patient's status may differ. The characteristics at onset, including activity, how the onset was noted, body po-

Part I Medical Nursing Care

sition at onset, and the rapidity with which maximal deficit developed are helpful in determining whether a stroke has occurred as well as the type of the stroke. For example, condition such as preceding TIAs which increase the likelihood of stroke by infarction as opposed to by hemorrhage. Changes in the level of consciousness at onset, the presence of severe headache or vomit, and the signs after onset are all very important since they can help to determine the type of stroke, its location, and the prognosis.

11.6 大脑中动脉狭窄
Middle Cerebral Artery Stenosis

背景/ Background

男性病人,62岁,患高血压、糖尿病12年。近一个多月头昏,左手麻木。

A 62-year-old male patient, who has been suffering from hypertension and diabetes mellitus for 12 years, had dizziness and numbness in his left hand for more than a month.

交流/ Interactions

检查者:你有什么不舒服?
Examiner: What kind of discomfort do you have?
病人:哦,头痛、头晕、记忆力差,左手麻木。
Patient: Oh, headache, vertigo, poor memory and numbness of my left hand.
检查者:这症状有多久了?
Examiner: How long have you had these symptoms?
病人:已超过一个月了。

第一部分　内科护患沟通

Patient: More than a month.

检查者：好，让我给你检查一下。

Examiner: All right. Let me give you an examination.

检查者：你以往生过什么病？

Examiner: What diseases have you had before?

病人：我50岁时查出患高血压和糖尿病。

Patient: I had hypertension and diabetes mellitus at the age of 50.

检查者：让我仔细查一下你的右侧颞窗。

Examiner: Let me examine your right temporal window carefully.

病人：我有问题吗？

Patient: Do I have any problem?

检查者：你的右侧大脑中动脉狭窄。

Examiner: There is a stenosis in your right middle cerebral artery.

病人：你认为我该怎么办？

Patient: What should I do?

检查者：你需要进一步做MRA或DSA检查。

Examiner: You should have a DSA or an MRA to confirm the findings.

病人：为什么？

Patient: Why?

检查者：它能显示颅内血管的形态学改变。

Examiner: These tests can show the shape changes of the intracranial blood vessels.

病人：那我的左手麻就是这个原因？

Patient: Did it cause the numbness in my left hand?

检查者：我认为是这样。这是你的检查报告，请给医生看。

Examiner: I think so. Here's your report. Please show it to your physician.

Part I Medical Nursing Care

点评 / Comments

　　大脑中动脉起始于颈内动脉分叉处。大脑中动脉第一段(M1 段)闭塞,几乎都会引起神经功能障碍。此处闭塞绝大多数由栓子引起。由于此种闭塞位于 Willis 环远端,故其侧支循环只能是大脑前、后动脉在脑表面吻合的血流。当这种侧枝血流不能建立时,M1 段闭塞可导致包括偏瘫、偏身感觉缺失、同向性偏盲和对侧凝视麻痹在内的严重神经功能缺失。如果梗死位于优势半球,还可出现失语。然而,大脑中动脉主干闭塞可因脑表面侧支循环丰富而发生所谓"巨大腔隙",主要引起运动功能障碍。

　　The middle cerebral artery begins at the bifurcation of internal carotid artery. Occlusion of the first portion of middle cerebral artery (M1 segment) almost always produces a neurological functional deficit. Most occlusions here are due to emboli. Since the occlusion is distal to the circle of Willis, the opportunity for collateral circulation is restricted to anastomotic blood flow from the anterior and posterior cerebral on the surface of the brain. When this fails, occlusion of the M1 segment results in a severe deficit including hemiplegia, hemisensory deficit, homonymous hemianopsia, contralateral gaze palsy, and aphasia, if the infarct is in the dominant hemisphere. However, occlusion of the middle cerebral artery stem may result primarily in a motor deficit due to the so-called giant lacune that occurs when there is over adequate collateral circulation on the brain surface.

第一部分　内科护患沟通

胰岛素的用药指导
Instructions on the Use of Insulin

施耀方

 背景/ *Background*

张女士,66 岁,有 2 型糖尿病史 12 年,长期服用格列齐特、美迪康、消渴丸等降糖药物治疗。近一年来血糖控制一直不理想,空腹血糖 12～13 mmol/L,餐后血糖 17～18 mmol/L。近阶段出现视物模糊、双下肢麻木症状。由于药物控制不佳,医生要求她住院改用胰岛素治疗。但护士小周了解到患者有顾虑,不愿意接受胰岛素治疗。在阅读了这位病人的病历资料、计划了教育内容后,小周来到病人床边。

Patient Ms. Zhang, 66 years old with 12 years of type-2 diabetes, has been taking Diamicron, Metformin and XiaoKe to lower her blood glucose level. Her blood glucose was poorly controlled in the past year with the fasting blood glucose ranging from 12～13 mmol/L and PBG ranging between 17～18 mmol/L. Recently, she is also suffering from visual blurring and lower extremity numbness. Because the above-mentioned medications were unsuccessful in controlling her levels, the patient was advised to be hospitalized for insulin treatment. Nurse Zhou understood that the patient had some concerns and did not like to have the insulin treatment. She reviewed the patient's medical records, developed a patient education

Part I Medical Nursing Care

plan, and approached the patient's bedside.

交流/ Interactions

护士:阿姨,您好,我是你的床位护士,我叫小周。我负责在您整个住院期间的护理工作,以后您不管碰到什么事,有什么需要我帮助的请尽管喊我。

Nurse: Hello, Ms. Zhang. I'm your nurse Miss Zhou. I will care for you during your stay at our hospital. You can call me whenever you need help.

病人:我现在的眼睛真是不行了,请你走近些让我看看清楚。我只能模糊地看出你的脸庞,连鼻眼也看不清楚。医生还要叫我打针,我连单位也看不清怎么打?

Patient: My vision is poor. Please come closer so I can see you better. I can only see your face, but I can't see your nose or eyes clearly. The doctor said I needed insulin injections, but I can hardly see the dosage. How can I give an injection by myself?

护士:张阿姨,您可能不知道吧,现在打胰岛素与以往是完全不一样了。不再需要您自己用针筒抽吸,胰岛素都是事先装配好的,您只要调节好单位,就可以打了。

Nurse: Ms. Zhang, you probably don't know that the way of injecting insulin is quite different from what it used to be. It's very easy now. The insulin is pre-mixed. You only need to adjust the units before using it.

病人:我根本看不见,怎么调啊?

Patient: But I cannot see it at all. How can I adjust it?

护士:我去拿个样品来,告诉您怎样使用。(周护士拿来了样品。)

Nurse: Let me get a sample, and show you how to use it. (Nurse Zhou brought over a sample device.)

护士:张阿姨,您摸摸看,它只比钢笔略粗一些。打的时候只要把笔轻轻摇动十几下,将里面的药液混匀后,您再摸摸笔的尾部有罗纹的地方,就是调节胰岛素的。您可以不用眼睛看,您听声音,每转动一

第一部分　内科护患沟通

下,听到一个咔嚓就是一个单位,您现在是打8个单位就是听到8个咔嚓(作示范状)。您听到了吗?这样胰岛素的单位就调节好了。

Nurse: Ms. Zhang, try to touch this. This is the device which is only a little bigger than a pen. Before using it, you need to shake it softly more than ten times to mix the insulin. You can change the units at the end of the device. You don't need to use your eyes. You can listen to the click sound. Each click means a unit. If you use 8 units, you need to hear 8 clicks (demonstration). Can you hear that? Now it is ready to be used.

病人:哦!这倒是蛮方便的,确实很简单。但我还是不想打针,我希望吃药控制。

Patient: Oh! It is easy. But I do not want to inject insulin. I would rather control my blood glucose with oral medication.

护士:能告诉我为什么吗?

Nurse: Can you tell me why?

病人:我听别人说,胰岛素这个东西是不能碰的。它就像毒品一样,一旦染上,就要终生依赖,再也戒不掉了。

Patient: Someone told me that insulin is like narcotics and once you use it you will have to depend on it for life.

护士:是别人说的,能告诉我这个"别人"是干什么的吗?

Nurse: Can you tell me who told you that?

病人:很多人都这么说的,我们一起喝茶、锻炼的老姐妹们说的。

Patient: Many people, including the women I exercise with.

护士:那么你说的"别人"都不是医生吧。我想治疗还是要相信科学。胰岛素发明了100多年,拯救了无数的生命。从原来的动物胰岛素发展到现在的人胰岛素,它的分子结钩、氨基酸排列完全与人胰岛素一致。我们的身体能分泌胰岛素,但是由于你体内分泌的胰岛素数量太少或不能正常发挥作用,那就需要外界补充胰岛素帮助你体内的胰岛素一起工作。

Nurse: They are not doctors, are they? We should believe in science. Insulin has been developed for over 100 years and many patients

Part I Medical Nursing Care

have benefited from it. From the development of animal insulin to human insulin, its molecular structure and amino acid sequence are the same as that of natural human insulin. Our body produces insulin, but when the insulin is not sufficiently produced on its own, then it's necessary for you to supplement the insulin from outside sources.

病人:那么就必须终生打胰岛素吗?

Patient: Do I need the injections all my life once I begin receiving the insulin?

护士:那要根据病情的发展情况。像你现在这样,吃了十几年的药,又出现了并发症,吃药对你来说作用不明显,那就必须打针。一般来说打3个月到半年的针,让您自己的胰岛细胞好好休息,等脚麻等并发症好转后,您仍可改为吃药。以后可能会吃药、打针交替进行,什么对您血糖控制有利,就用什么方法。

Nurse: It depends on your condition. It is appropriate for you to use insulin now because you have used anti-diabetic drugs for more than ten years, currently it is not effective, and complications have occurred. You can use insulin for 3 to 6 months to allow the B cells of your pancreas to rest. And you can stop using it if your condition improves. It can be a combination of both oral medication and injection. Which method will be used depends on the effect of the glucose control.

病人:听你这么一说,我就放心多了,那我先打一段时间针。

Patient: Oh, I understand. I will take the insulin injection now.

护士:您一定要注意,在注射胰岛素后半个小时一定要吃饭,不能太早,也不能延迟。如果出现心慌、出冷汗,可能是低血糖的表现,您一定要打铃告诉我们。另外,您的床头柜内需要准备一包苏打饼干,以备低血糖时用。不过您放心,这只是作预防用,医生和护士们在治疗过程中会密切监测您的血糖的。

Nurse: You need to be very careful once you start using insulin. You have to eat something 30 minutes after using insulin. Don't eat it too early or too late. If you feel palpitations and perspiration, you must ring the bell

第一部分　内科护患沟通

and call us. It could be symptoms of hypoglycemia. There are some cookies in your bedside cabinet which are prepared for you in the case of hypoglycemia. But you don't need to worry about it. It's just a precaution. Doctors and nurses will monitor your blood glucose closely during the treatment process.

病人：好的！谢谢你，周护士，我会配合你们治疗的。等打针的时候还要麻烦你教教我。

Patient: Thanks a lot. I will do as you tell me. Could you be so kind as to remind me how to use the injection device again later?

护士：放心吧，您肯定能学会的，到时我一定教您学会全部操作。我现在还要去看别的病人，先走了，有什么事尽管找我。

Nurse: OK. Don't worry. I promise that I will teach you until you are able to handle the whole procedure. I have to see some other patients now, so I'll see you later. Goodbye.

点评 / *Comments*

2型糖尿病病人在口服药效果不好出现并发症时，需要应用胰岛素治疗。但是有较多的糖尿病患者对胰岛素治疗的顾虑很多，有一种广为流传的说法是：胰岛素是毒品，一经沾上必将终生依赖。还有一些患者认为，打针特别麻烦，外出旅行、出差、工作都不方便，而且打针很痛。实际上这只是对糖尿病的知识及胰岛素认识的缺乏。现在注射胰岛素使用的是胰岛素注射笔，非常方便，设计也具人性化，外观像一支笔。胰岛素在常温下可以放置一个月，注射用的针是世界上最细的针，只有0.30 mm，长度为8 mm，注射无痛感，携带方便，因此对患者外出、旅行都不会造成不便。总之，这次糖尿病健康教育进行得非常好，护理人员用科学知识深入浅出、形象生动地说服了护理对象，用事实打消了病人的顾虑，心悦诚服地配合治疗。这充分说明了健康教育是一种对身心疾病重要和有效易行的护理手段。

When Type 2 diabetes is not controlled by oral drugs and complications occur, insulin should be used. A considerable number of patients

Part I Medical Nursing Care

have misgivings about insulin treatment, believing that insulin is poisonous and addictive, and may need to be used for one's whole life while others think that the injection is cumbersome and painful and not convenient in case of travel. Such beliefs are misleading and mostly related to ignorance. The fact is that modern insulin injectors are very handy with a 0.30 mm diameter and 8 mm long painless needle. Insulin can be stored at room temperature for a month, so it poses no inconvenience for travel. In this episode, the diabetes health education was conducted very well. The nurse was able to convince the patient with scientific knowledge and demonstrated the proper use of the insulin injector, and thus alleviated the patient's worries. The patient cooperated willingly with the treatment. This shows that health education is an important and effective nursing strategy to care for the mind and body of the patient.

第一部分　内科护患沟通

I-13

糖尿病病人的择医指导
Instructions on Treatment Selection for a Diabetic Patient

施耀方

背景/ Background

患者倪某,男,66岁,有2型糖尿病史5年,以往服用格列齐特、美迪康等降糖药物治疗。2年前由别人介绍参加了异教组织"法轮功",相信通过练功可以使身体强壮。练功后有病不能上医院,不能吃药,只要相信大师的法力,每天坚持练功就可以祛除任何疾病。倪先生经洗脑及练功后逐渐走火入魔,停用任何药物。其夫人也受其影响参信魔法。倪先生不再上医院测血糖、检查。一周前,患者出现发热、寒颤却仍在家坚持练功,不吃药、不看病。夫妻俩坚信大师一定会来拯救他们的。结果被回家探视他的女儿强行送入医院。患者来院时已呈昏迷状态,血糖达 34 mmol/L,体温 40.2℃,重度脱水。立即给予输液、抗感染、降血糖治疗。经过两天两夜的抢救,患者终于清醒,脱离危险状态。床位护士小吴与之聊了起来。

Patient Ni, male, 66 years old, had Type 2 Diabetes for 5 years. He used to take Diamicron and Metformin to control the disease. Two years ago he was introduced to and joined the controversial "Fa-Lun-Gong"

Part I Medical Nursing Care

Cult. He believed he could get rid of all diseases solely by practicing "Fa-Lun-Da-Fa" if he put his trust in the Master of the faith. In addition, he was forbidden to seek help from doctors or use medication. After practicing the cult exercise for some time, Mr. Li stopped taking all medicine. He also influenced his wife to join the controversial faction. Mr. Ni has not visited the hospital since and has not taken a blood glucose test. One week ago, Mr. Ni developed a high fever and chills. But he still kept practicing "Fa-Lun-Gong" at home and refused to go to the hospital or take drugs. They believed the Master would surely come to save them. Badly dehydrated and in coma, he was rushed to the hospital by his daughter who happened to drop by to visit them. His blood glucose test showed 34 mmol/L, and his body temperature was 40.2℃. Treated with fluid infusion, anti-inflammation drugs and insulin, he regained consciousness 48 hours later. Miss Wu, the nurse who took care of him had a conversation with him then.

交流/ *Interactions*

护士：倪先生,你可醒了,把你的夫人和女儿吓坏了,感觉怎么样?

Nurse: Mr. Ni, it's nice to see you have come around. Your wife and daughter were scared to death. How do you feel?

病人：就是没有力气,不想动。

Patient: I'm exhausted and I don't feel like moving at all.

护士：没关系的,你好好休息,我来告诉你,今天的血糖已降到18.6 mmol/L。我来帮你测个体温。现在是38.0℃。很好,你现在要多喝水,每小时要喝掉这么一杯,大约是100 mL。你能喝水就可以少挂水,可以减轻心脏负担。

Nurse: Don't worry and make sure you have a good rest. Your blood glucose has decreased to 18.6 mmol/L today. Let me take your body temperature. Oh, very good, 38.0℃. You should drink one glass of water, about 100 mL every hour. You will need less fluid infusion if you can drink more water. It can decrease the workload on your heart.

病人:好的,我尽量喝。

Patient: OK. I will try.

护士:你先休息吧,过会我来看你。

Nurse: Have a rest. I will see you later.

病人:谢谢。

Patient: Thank you.

(又过了 2 天,倪先生已基本恢复,体温 37.5 ℃。空腹血糖 10.6 mmol/L。)

(Two days later, Mr. Ni recovered almost completely, with temperature of 37.5℃ and fasting blood glucose of 10.6 mmol/L.)

护士:倪先生,你今天气色真好。我现在给你测定餐后 2 小时血糖,是 15.4 mmol/L。

Nurse: Mr. Ni, you look very well today. Now let me measure your 2-hour-after-meal blood glucose. Well, it's 15.4 mmol/L.

病人:为什么餐后比空腹要高那么多?

Patient: Why is the blood glucose level always much higher after meals?

护士:这是 2 型糖尿病的特点。由于你的胰岛素功能差,食物吸收以后,没有足够的胰岛素把血糖降下来,因此餐后的血糖会比空腹高很多。

Nurse: It's one of the characteristics of Type 2 Diabetes. Because of the malfunction of your islet, there isn't enough insulin to decrease your blood glucose which leads to higher post-meal blood glucose.

病人:原来是这样。那有什么办法降下来吗?

Patient: I see. Is there any way to decrease it?

护士:你只要坚持正规用药,血糖是可以降下来的。像你原来那样不吃药、不治疗是不行的。

Nurse: Yes. It will surely drop back to normal range if you keep taking the medicine. It is not good if you don't follow the treatment or take the

Part I   Medical Nursing Care

medication.

病人：可是我的感觉真的是很好，没有任何的不舒服。

Patient: But I feel pretty well these days, nothing uncomfortable.

护士：这又是2型糖尿病的特点。在早期可以没有任何不适，等到出现并发症时才发现有糖尿病。餐后高血糖的危害是非常大的，会对人的心脏、血管、神经产生损害，比如你的尿液检查表明肾脏已有损害，明天再去做个眼底检查。

Nurse: This is another characteristic of Type II Diabetes. Patients usually feel nothing is wrong in the early stage. Some people don't realize until complications occur. The post-meal hyperglycemia will do great harm to the patient's heart, blood vessels and nerves. For example, your urine test shows your kidneys have some damage. You should have your retina checked tomorrow.

病人：好的。

Patient: OK.

护士：倪先生，你的眼底检查结果出来了，你的眼底病变比较严重了，需要手术治疗，等你的血糖降下来就可以手术了。

Nurse: Mr. Ni, here is the result of your retina examination. Your retina problem is serious. You should have an operation when your blood glucose drops to normal.

病人：有这么严重？不过我的眼睛看不清已经有一年多了，我以为是老花了也没在意。

Patient: That serious? I've had a very bad eyesight for more than a year. I thought it was an aging-related problem.

护士：你的眼睛是由于糖尿病长期血糖控制不佳引起的眼底病变，必须要手术治疗，治疗后的效果是比较好的，但是你的血糖必须控制好。

Nurse: The retina damage results from long periods of poor blood glucose control. An operation is necessary. It will improve your eyesight a lot. But first you must keep your blood glucose in a normal range.

第一部分　内科护患沟通

病人：后果真的很严重,我原来一点也不懂。听别人说练功后可以治疗疾病,我想糖尿病是慢性病,练了功可以不吃药,省了很多麻烦又可以强身,一举两得,看来是耽误了自己的治疗,引来了不必要的身体伤害。

Patient: I didn't realize it was so severe. I was told "Fa-Lun-Gong" could cure my disease. Considering diabetes is a chronic disease, I thought I could get rid of the medication, improve my heath and avoid trouble if I kept practicing it. Now I recognize that because I've delayed my treatment, it has led to more damage to my health.

护士：是的,糖尿病是一种终身性疾病,目前尚无办法根治,只有靠药物长期控制预防并发症。不要让任何信仰说服你不服药。从现在起你只要坚持治疗,把血糖控制住,还能像正常人一样生活。

Nurse: Yes. Diabetes is a life-long disease, which cannot be cured completely at the present time. But complications can be prevented by means of medication. If you can stick to the treatment and keep your blood glucose under control from now on, you should be able to live normally just like others.

病人：看来人是需要活到老学到老,我会记住这次教训,相信科学,相信医生,坚持终身治疗。

Patient: It seems the old saying "one is never too old to learn" is correct. I will keep this in mind. I will believe in science and the doctors, and stick to medical treatment for the rest of my life.

点评/ Comments

俗话说"久病乱投医",这是很多慢性病病人的共有特征。由于长期疾病缠身,迁延不愈,使他们深受病痛折磨,又急于摆脱疾病对生命的威胁,常会求治心切,甚至到处打听和寻觅偏方、验方和土方法,希望有朝一日能找到治愈其病痛的灵丹妙药,以致倪先生让"法轮功"引入歧途。护理人员必须用科学知识去准确引导,用真诚感情帮助患者树立信心,以理智和热情经常进行教育,以事实让他们相信科学,促使

Part I Medical Nursing Care

病人早日康复。

The common saying "disorderly beg to cure the long term illness" is a characteristic of many patients with chronic diseases. The patients are eager to get rid of diseases by seeking special prescriptions everywhere. Mr. Ni was led astray by "Fa-Lun-Gong". The nursing staff must persuade their patients with scientific knowledge, and help them gain confidence with sincere affection and passion. This kind of health education, conducted with facts and knowledge, will lead patients to believe in science and help them overcome their illnesses.

第一部分　内科护患沟通

糖尿病病人的饮食指导
Dietary Instructions for a Patient with Diabetes Mellitus

李惠玲

背景 / Background

李先生,70岁,糖尿病合并白内障,嗜酒。他入院后仍偷偷饮酒及吃甜食。责任护士发现后来到李先生床边,开始了他们的谈话。

Mr. Li, 70 years old, has diabetes complicated with cataracts and likes to drink alcohol. He continued to drink alcohol and eat desserts even after admission to the hospital. The nurse in charge came to Mr. Li's bedside and had the following conversation.

交流 / Interactions

护士：李先生,我听说您很爱甜食和饮酒,是吗?

Nurse：Mr. Li, I've heard that you are fond of desserts and alcohol, right?

病人：是的,没喝酒我就睡不着觉。我知道患糖尿病不能喝酒,可是我就是挡不住酒的诱惑。

Patient：Yes, I can't go to sleep without a drink. I know that diabetes

Part I Medical Nursing Care

patients should not drink, but I just can't resist the temptation of wine.

护士:您现在的血糖处于高水平,又并发了白内障,如果再不禁酒,不控制甜食,并发症会更多、更重。我们能否想个办法共同努力控制酒欲和甜食呢?

Nurse: Right now your blood glucose is high and you also have cataracts. If you don't give up drinking and don't stop eating desserts, complications will become worse. Why don't we find a way together to curb your desire for wine and desserts?

病人:好的,我正需要你的指导和帮助。

Patient: That's fine. What I need are your instructions and help.

护士:那好,让我们来找一些有兴趣的事做,像听音乐、下棋、看小说等等,分散您对酒和甜食的注意力。然后我们为你订个合理的食谱,让营养师替您加工得色香味俱全,刺激您对食物的欲望,相信您会有能力控制酒和甜食的。

Nurse: Then let's find some interesting things like listening to music, playing chess or reading novels to divert your attention from alcohol and desserts. We can plan an appropriate diet menu for you. We can also request that the nutritionist prepare food with good color, aroma, and flavor for you to stimulate your appetite. I'm sure you are capable of controlling wine and desserts intake.

病人:行,我一定努力合作。还有一个问题想请教一下,我的双眼都患了白内障,左眼几乎全看不见了,右眼的视力也很差,使我行动非常不便,不知能否治好?

Patient: Sure, I'll do my best to cooperate with you. Another question is that I have cataracts in both of my eyes. My left eye is almost totally blind and the eyesight of my right eye is very poor. This makes it very inconvenient for me to get around. Can they be treated?

护士:可以治的,只要血糖控制正常了,我们可以请眼科医师来给您会诊,一般只需做一简单手术(激光或超声雾化)就能帮您重见光明的。

第一部分　内科护患沟通

Nurse: They can be treated. We can ask the eye doctor to see you after your blood glucose level becomes normal. A simple operation (laser beam or ultrasonic therapy) will enable you to see again.

病人：太好了,我一定好好配合你们尽快控制血糖,争取早日安排眼科手术。

Patient: That's great. I'll cooperate with you to have my blood glucose controlled and then schedule for the eye operation as soon as possible.

护士：好,让我们共同努力。

Nurse: Fine. Let's work hard together.

结果 / Result

李先生两周后血糖降至正常,并转眼科顺利接受白内障手术。术后一周出院。

Mr. Li's blood glucose became normal after two weeks. He was transferred to the Ophthalmology Department, and was discharged one week after the successful cataract surgery.

Part Ⅰ　Medical Nursing Care

癌症病人化疗前的护理
Nursing Care for a Cancer Patient before Chemotherapy

金美娟

背景/ Background

因乳房癌术后一个月要行静脉化疗的沈女士，听说化疗会引起恶心、呕吐、脱发等副作用，非常紧张，她怕不能坚持治疗。这时，床位护士小许来到她的身边。

Ms. Shen had a breast cancer operation last month. She is going to receive further treatment via intravenous chemotherapy. She became very nervous when hearing that chemotherapy may cause vomiting and alopecia. She feared that she may not be able to withstand the treatment procedure. At this time, Miss Xu, her primary nurse came to care for her.

交流/ Interactions

病人：小许，我很害怕。本来以为肿块切除了，现在恢复得不错，也就好了，没想到还要化疗。化疗又有很多副作用，我怕我不能坚持治疗。

Patient：Miss Xu, I am really afraid. Originally, I thought I would be

第一部分　内科护患沟通

healed once the tumor was surgically removed. I never thought that I would need chemotherapy which has many adverse effects. I am afraid I will not be able to persist in this treatment.

护士：手术是肿瘤治疗的主要手段之一,化疗也是目前主要的辅助治疗。术后为了预防及控制癌细胞的扩散或浸润,进行化疗是非常必要的。化疗也就是应用化学药物治疗的方法。比起手术来说,化疗带来的副作用应该容易克服得多。好比爬山,虽然这一路会有很多困难,但只要勇敢面对,坚持下去,一定能达到顶点,看到美丽的风景。化疗也是一样。况且,我们会帮助您的。

Nurse: Surgery is one of the major methods of oncotherapy, while chemotherapy is also a main treatment technology at the present time. It is absolutely necessary to carry out chemotherapy after the surgery to prevent and control the spread or infiltration of the cancer cells. Chemotherapy is a treatment method of using chemicals to control the cancer cells. Compared to surgery, the side effects of chemotherapy should be overcome more easily. It is like climbing a mountain, you will encounter a great deal of difficulties on the way, but if you bravely confront these difficulties, and persist in climbing, you can surely reach the top and view the beautiful scenery. Chemotherapy works the same way for cancer. Besides, we will help you during the whole process.

病人：那化疗到底有哪些副作用?

Patient: What side effects chemotherapy will have?

护士：化疗有很多副作用,包括胃肠道反应,如恶心、呕吐、便秘;过敏反应;骨髓抑制,如白细胞、血小板下降;肝功能损害;脱发等。但不是所有副作用都会出现,也不是每个人都有。

Nurse: Chemotherapy has many side effects including gastrointestinal tract reactions such as nausea, vomiting, and constipation; allergic responses; bone marrow depression as white blood cells and platelet counts drop off; damage of liver function; and alopecia. But, not all side effects will occur and not all patients have the same side effects.

Part I   Medical Nursing Care

病人：那怎么来预防这些副作用？

Patient: How can these side effects be prevented?

护士：化疗前,我们会给您做全面的检查,如验血的指标、拍摄CT、查心电图等。了解您的全身情况及肿瘤情况,选择效果较好、副作用相对较轻的方案。具体的,床位医生会详细跟您谈的。最主要的,医生会进行化疗前的预处理,也就是使用一些预防呕吐、过敏、保护肝功能的药物,最大程度地减轻药物的副作用。另外,合理的饮食、良好的情绪、充足的睡眠也是非常重要的。可以说,经过预处理,大部分病人出现的副作用是轻微的,所以,您不用害怕。

Nurse: Before chemotherapy, we will run several examinations for you, including blood test, CT, electrocardiogram, etc. to understand your body and your tumor conditions. We will select the most effective treatment plan with the least side effects for you. Your doctor will discuss the detailed plan with you. The doctor will carry out pre-treatment for you before the chemotherapy by using some drugs to prevent vomiting, allergic reactions, and to protect your liver function. In addition, reasonable food and drinks, good attitude and enough sleep are very important, too. The majority of the patients receiving chemotherapy have only minimal side effects after pre-treatment. Therefore you don't have to worry.

病人：那要脱发吗？

Patient: Well, how about losing hair?

护士：化疗不一定都会脱发。它主要与使用某些药物有关,大部分药物是不会引起脱发的。脱发,也只是暂时的,停药以后,头发就自然长好了,同时,也存在着个体差异。即使出现脱发,也可以戴发套、戴帽子或扎丝巾,同样非常漂亮的。关于这个问题,您先生已有充分的思想准备,我们已经交流过了,您不用担心。在治疗过程中,我还会具体地给您讲解,与您交流,希望我们合作得很好。

Nurse: Hair loss does not occur with all chemotherapy patients. Whether or not you lose your hair depends on the specific drugs and their dosages administered. Most drugs don't cause hair loss and there are individual differences to chemotherapy as well. Also, chemotherapy inducing hair loss is temporary and your hair will start to grow back once the treatment is finished. If you lose your hair, you can use a wig, hat, or scarf to protect your scalp. You will look beautiful when you use them. It's not necessary for you to worry about hair loss because we have discussed this possibility with your husband and he has already had enough mental preparation for it. During the treatment, we will tell you all the details about the therapy. We can exchange thoughts with each other and hopefully you can cooperate with us.

病人:真的?谢谢你,小许。

Patient: Really? Thanks, Miss Xu.

结果 / Result

沈女士了解了化疗的相关知识,很顺利地完成了第一次化疗,无明显恶心、呕吐等不良反应,对轻微的脱发也能坦然接受。沈女士表示,接下来的疗程会充满信心,以最佳的状态坚持治疗。

Ms. Shen learned about chemotherapy and finished the first session successfully. She had no symptom of nausea and vomiting and was able to accept the slight hair loss. She said that she had enough confidence in the treatment process and would continue to receive the remaining sessions full of hope.

点评 / Comments

"希望和焦虑并存"是肿瘤病人的心理特征之一。他们都在为肿瘤病本身所带来的痛苦或治疗过程中的不适而担忧,又希望通过治疗和护理后能治愈疾病和延长生命。护理人员对他们的"心理支持"则是减轻焦虑、提升希望的最有效措施之一。心理支持的核心是理解、同情、关爱、鼓励和提供力所能及的帮助。本案例针对沈女士在化疗后,可能出现脱发而导致自我形象的破坏这一关键心理问题进行认知领悟、启发,引导她在健康和自我形象两者之间做了正确选择。在改

Part I Medical Nursing Care

变认知的基础上,才能真正自我接纳和重塑,完成治疗过程。

"Hope and anxiety exist simultaneously" is one of the psychological characteristics of cancer patients. The patients are worried about the pain from the disease and the treatment process, and at the same time wish to be cured and prolong their lives after treatment and nursing care. For them, the "psychological support" from the nursing personnel is one of the most effective measures to relieve their anxieties and to promote their hopes. The core of psychological support is comprehension, sympathy, caring, encouragement and to offer help within our power. From the above episode, we know that Ms. Shen was concerned about the destruction of her self-image because of the potential hair loss caused by chemotherapy. She made the right choice between health and self-image after being inspired, enlightened, and guided by the nurse. Based on her perceptional changes, the patient became accepting, reestablished herself, and completed the chemotherapy.

第二部分 外科护患沟通
Part II Surgical Nursing Care

第二部分　外科护患沟通

颈椎骨折术后复健
Post-operative Rehabilitation for a Patient with Fractured Cervical Spine

张妍

背景/ Background

女性病人，车祸致 C5-6 骨折伴截瘫入院，行颅骨牵引后 3 天手术，术后肢三角肌、肱二头肌、肱三头肌肌力Ⅲ级，双手握力弱，右足趾能自主背伸但是运动费力，双膝关节及左足趾无明显活动。手术第二天，床位护士小刘准备为她进行功能锻炼。

A female patient, suffered from a C5 and C6 fracture and paraplegia because of an automobile accident. She was hospitalized and received surgery after 3 days of cranial skeletal traction. The strength of the deltoid, biceps and triceps muscles were level 3, the grasping force of the hands was weak and the right toes could extend, but the patient needed to use great effort. The left toes and both knees had no active movement. The second day after the surgery, Nurse Liu went to the patient and tried to perform the functional training.

Part II Surgical Nursing Care

交流 / *Interactions*

护士：你好！昨晚睡得好吗？

Nurse: How are you? Did you sleep well last night?

病人：睡得很好！手术以后我就安心了许多。

Patient: Yes. I feel at ease after the surgery.

护士：现在手术做好了，接下来最重要的就是功能锻炼了。今天开始你就要进行有计划的功能锻炼，每天由我来指导你，请配合！

Nurse: The surgery was a success. From now on, the most important thing we can do is the functional training. I'll teach you each day. Please follow my instructions.

病人：谢谢，我一定会努力的。

Patient: Thank you. I'll try my best.

护士：那好，我们先来做第一个动作，双上肢上举抓住吊环，每天100次，可以分4~5个时间段进行。

Nurse: OK, let's begin. Raise your arms and grasp the rings. You should do this at least 100 times every day. You may divide them into 4 or 5 sessions.

病人：好。（努力举起双臂）我感觉双上肢特别重。

Patient: OK. (making great efforts to raise her arms) My arms feel so heavy.

护士：这是刚开始锻炼时的感觉，以后你会感觉越来越轻松的。

Nurse: You will have this feeling in the first several days, but it will get easier later.

病人：（双手抓不住吊环）不行了，我怎么会觉得大脑支配不了我的双手了？

Patient: (can't hold on the rings) I can't do it. It seems that my brain can't control my hands.

第二部分　外科护患沟通

护士：这就是颈椎受伤后神经受损的表现，只有每天坚持练习，才能恢复功能。这个动作现在对你来说有一定的难度，那我们换一种方法。现在我给你一个小矿泉水瓶，你用双手争取把它抓住，然后在两手间传递，这样行吗？

Nurse: This is the phenomenon of the injured nerve caused by fracture of the cervical spine. The only way you can recover the function of the nerve is doing daily training. It looks like this exercise is too hard for you now, so let's change to another. I will give you a small water bottle. You try to hold it and pass it between your two hands. Can you do that?

病人：(双手练习握矿泉水瓶)哎,这个办法真好。

Patient: (practicing to pass the water bottle) Oh, this method is better.

护士：这样每天坚持到疲劳为止。(锻炼5分钟后)你有点累了吧？现在让你稍做休息，我帮你做下肢膝关节和踝关节的被动运动。你自己不能动的关节都要像这样的被动运动，有时间可请护理员或家属协助帮你运动，这样才能保持关节的功能。

Nurse: You should continue the exercise until you are tired. (after 5 minutes of exercise) Do you feel tired now? You can take a rest. I'll do some passive movements for your knees and ankles. The joints that you can't move by yourself will need this kind of passive movement. You can ask your family members or paramedics to help you. This exercise can help the function of your knees and ankles.

病人：好的,我会经常练习的。

Patient: OK, I'll do the exercise frequently.

护士：下面我再帮助你锻炼足趾背伸运动,自己努力翘足趾。(5秒钟后右足趾稍微动了一下)对,很好,就像那样继续活动足趾。

Nurse: Now let me help you do the toe extension exercise. Try your best to extend the toes. (5 seconds later, the patient's right toes have an

Part II Surgical Nursing Care

inconspicuous movement.) Yes, very good, continue to move your toes like that.

病人:太费力了,我几乎用了全身的劲了。

Patient: Oh, my gosh, it almost requires all my strength.

护士:但通过你的努力,脚趾确实动起来了,这就是良好的开端,只要你坚持下去你恢复的希望很大,因为你是我见过的最坚强的女性。

Nurse: But with your effort, the toes actually moved. It's a good beginning. You have the great possibility of recovery if you persist. You are the most determined woman I have ever met.

病人:太谢谢了,你让我看到康复的希望。

Patient: Thank you very much. You give me the hope of recovery.

护士:相信你康复后会走着来看我们的。我们期待着这一天。

Nurse: I believe you will walk back to visit us after you've completed recovery. We are looking forward to that moment.

结果/ *Result*

在责任护士的指导下,病人坚持四肢功能锻炼。两周后,双上肢活动自如,手能握住并举起装 100 ml 的矿泉水瓶,右下肢踝关节可自主活动,右足趾背伸力好,右膝关节能轻微活动,左下肢足趾活动微弱,患者对康复充满信心。

Under the guidance of the primary nurse, the patient exercised her limbs persistently. Two weeks later, the patient's two arms had free movement; her two hands could hold and raise a bottle filled with 100 ml of water; her right ankle could move freely; the extension strength of her right toes was good; her right knee and left toes had slight movement, and the patient had full confidence on rehabilitation.

第二部分 外科护患沟通

点评 / 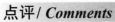Comments

这段情景对话描写护士使病人感受到关心、爱护,有安全感并且树立了自信心。护士用充满热情的话语和适当的指导和鼓励使病人获得希望、勇气和力量,从而加快疾病的康复。

This episode showed that the nurse made the patient feel that she had been cared and loved. She was safe, and established her self-confidence. The nurse did this with warm speech, proper guidance and encouragement. This made the patient regain her hope, courage and strength and accelerated the patient's rehabilitation.

Part Ⅱ   Surgical Nursing Care

肌无力病人在气管切开前的恐惧
A Myasthenia Patient's Fear before Tracheotomy

苏翠红

病人杨某,男性,66岁,因重症肌力危象而于深夜急诊入院。给予新斯的明肌注,症状无改善,继而出现面色、口唇明显紫绀,呼吸浅促,费力,达36次/分,需紧急行气管切开术。已请来五官科、麻醉科主任医师准备施行手术,协助患者取好去枕、肩部垫高仰卧位。但患者因强烈的濒死感,情绪紧张,出现挣扎,致气切手术无法正常进行。在这紧急状态下,护士轻轻地握住患者的手。

Patient Mr. Yang, 66 years old, had an emergency admission late at night because of a myasthenia crisis. After being given intramuscular neostigmine, his symptoms had not improved. He had clearly cyanosed lips and complexion, and shallow rapid respiration at the rate of 36 times per minute. An urgent tracheotomy was needed. Doctors of the ENT and anesthetic departments were summoned to perform the operation. The patient was assisted to lie in a supine position without a pillow or shoulder support. Since the patient sensed that he might be dying, he became extremely nervous and began to flounder. The operation could not be processed normally due to his restlessness. At this critical time, the nurse took the patient's hands and held them gently.

交流/ *Interactions*

护士：老杨,我知道你现在很难受。你看,我们大家都在竭尽全力想办法,希望使你早些摆脱目前的状况。你所要做的就是躺下来,尽量保持体位不要动。

Nurse: Mr. Yang, I know you are feeling very bad right now. We'll try our best to free you from your current status. What you should do now is to lie down, maintain the same body position, and don't move.

病人：不行,我不能睡平,躺下去我怕我就起不来了。

Patient: No, I can't lie down flat. I'm afraid that if I lie down, I won't be able to get up again.

护士：老杨,气管切开是解决你目前问题的最好的,也是唯一的办法。你看,我们医院五官科、麻醉科最好的主任医师都是深夜从家中赶来,就是想挽救你的生命。你放心,绝对没事的,你只需坚持配合好几分钟,就行了。

Nurse: Mr. Yang, tracheotomy is the best and only way to solve your problem at present. Our best physicians of the ENT and anesthetic departments rushed here from home late at night to save your life. Relax, it's absolutely no problem. Cooperate with us for several minutes and it will be over.

病人：不行,我还是睡不下去,我会死的。

Patient: No, I still can't lie down. I will die.

护士：老杨,不要害怕。手术过程中,我会一直在你身边的。而且你看,呼吸机我都已经为你准备在床边了,即使你真的没有自主呼吸了,这个机器也会帮助你呼吸的。你决不会死的,我保证。

Nurse: Mr. Yang, don't be afraid. During the operation, I will stay with you the whole time. Furthermore, the respirator has been prepared

Part Ⅱ　Surgical Nursing Care

and placed beside your bed. If you can't breathe by yourself, the machine can help you breathe. I guarantee that you won't die.

病人：是吗,我不会死吗？我儿子在哪儿？

Patient：Really? I won't die? Where is my son?

护士：老杨,这么多好医师在这儿,你决不会死的。(同时紧紧地握了一下患者的手。)你儿子在这儿呢。老杨,握住你儿子的手,让我们共同度过这个关键时刻,好吗？

Nurse：Mr. Yang, there are so many good doctors here. You will not die. (The nurse held his hand tightly.) Here is your son, Mr. Yang. Hold his hand, and let's get through this together, OK?

(老杨点了点头,他儿子跪在床边紧紧地握住父亲的手,同时在五官科主任的示意下我们先为患者静推了 10 mg 安定,并马上配合施行了气切术,为患者连接了人工呼吸机辅助呼吸。当一切就绪后,患者在辅助呼吸下,呼吸畅通了,紫绀消失了,脸上露出了疲惫的、放松的微笑,慢慢地睡着了。)

(Mr. Yang nodded. His son kneeled down at the bedside keeping his father's hand in his grasp. At the same time with the advice of the head of the ENT department, the doctors gave the patient 10 mg of Valium intravenously, performed the tracheotomy immediately, and connected the respirator to the patient to assist his breathing. After all was done, the patient's purple complexion disappeared gradually. He breathed without difficulty, and fell asleep with an exhausted but relaxed smile on his face.)

点评 / *Comments*

由于自感病情严重而导致精神上的极度不安,这是危重病人共有的心理特征。他们感觉濒临死亡,既希望得到即刻的救治,又害怕因医护人员处理不当而造成严重后果。护理人员应洞悉病人及家属的这种矛盾心情,用沉着和切境的语言进行安慰和疏导,取得护理对象的信任和配合,同时以果断和熟练的技术赢得治疗时机,争取抢救成功。

第二部分 外科护患沟通

Extreme fear from awareness of the severity of the disease is the common psychological characteristic of critically ill patients. Feeling close to death, they are not only longing for an immediate treatment, but also are afraid of the serious consequences that may result from improper treatment by doctors and nurses. Nurses should be aware of the concerns of the patients and their families. Nurses must provide comfort and guidance to obtain the patients' trust and cooperation by using calm and appropriate words. At the same time, nurses also need to grab the opportunity for emergency interventions with decisive and skillful techniques to help patients obtain successful treatment.

Part Ⅱ Surgical Nursing Care

Ⅱ-3

高位截瘫病人的整体护理
Holistic Nursing Care for a High-level Paraplegia Patient

李惠玲

 背景/ *Background*

病人梁先生,男性,30岁,因骑摩托车发生车祸后致胸、腰椎骨折。入院诊断:高位截瘫。病人神志清楚,精神沮丧,二便失禁,不能坐立。新婚3个月的妻子赵某来院见状忧虑不安,一个完整的家庭面临着危机。此时,责任护士来到了病人和他妻子的身边,向他们伸出了援助之手。

Patient Mr. Liang, 30 years old, fractured his thoracolumbar vertebra in a motorcycle accident. The hospital admission diagnosis was high paraplegia. The patient was conscious, sad, had incontinence of stool and urine, and could not sit or stand. His wife arrived at the hospital in a hurry and was very concerned. The young couple got married only three months ago. The whole family faced a crisis. The nurse-in-charge went to the patient and his wife and tried to give them a hand.

第二部分　外科护患沟通

交流 / Interactions

护士：梁先生,请您张开嘴,给您漱漱口,好吗?

Nurse：Mr. Liang, please open your mouth and let me brush your teeth, OK?

病人：(沮丧地)不必了。

Patient：(sadly) No, there is no need.

护士：您现在的状况确实使大家都很痛苦,但并不是毫无希望呀!后天主任就要给您动手术进行复位。您的状况对手术会有一定影响。告诉我您在想什么,让我来为您分担些,好吗?

Nurse：The situation of your health makes everyone feel sad, but there is still hope. The chief doctor is going to perform the operation on you the day after tomorrow. Your attitude will have an influence on the success of the operation. Please tell me what you are thinking and let me share your concerns, OK?

病人：手术会让我重新站起来吗?希望有多少,告诉我实话。

Patient：Can I stand up again after the operation? Just tell me the truth, please.

护士：好的。脊柱外科手术在国内发展得很快。给您做手术的医生又是国内最权威的,只要您有信心并积极配合,术后肯定比现在的状况要好,起码知觉要多一些,并且能坐起来,像张海迪那样坐在轮椅上不一样能成为强者吗?

Nurse：Spinal surgery techniques have progressed very quickly in our country and the doctor who will perform the operation on you is a noted authority in this field. Your condition will definitely become better after the operation. Your tactile sensibility will be improved. At least you can sit in the wheelchair like Mrs. Zhang Haidi. You will still be a healthy man if you believe you can do it and cooperate with us.

病人：好吧。(病人张开了嘴,护士为他做口腔护理。)

Patient：OK. (The patient opened his mouth and the nurse did the

Part Ⅱ Surgical Nursing Care

oralcare for him).

护士:漱完口您该吃早餐了。赵小姐(病人的妻子),你来喂他,好吗?

Nurse: Now you may have your breakfast. Mrs. Liang, you can feed him now.

病人:好的。(赵小姐开始细心地喂病人早餐,护士暂离。)

Patient: OK. (Mrs. Liang began to feed the patient carefully and the nurse left.)

(下午,病人妻子突然找到责任护士,说病人的导尿管脱落了,需要重插。责任护士找来了床位医生为病人重新插好导尿管并给予指导。)

(That afternoon, Mrs. Liang went to the nurse and told her that her husband's urinary catheter had slipped out and it needed to be reinserted. The nurse asked the doctor in charge to come to reinsert the catheter for the patient and also to give him some instructions.)

护士:尿管只能暂时缓解病人腹胀,但不能"依赖它"。最好每两小时夹管半小时,让病人的膀胱充盈,培养其排尿的条件反射,这样及早锻炼能促进自己控制排尿,您的负担就减轻了。怎么样?试着练几次,好吗?

Nurse: The catheter can temporarily relieve the patient's abdominal distention. But, we should not rely on it forever. We should clamp it for half an hour every two hours, to fill the bladder, and train the urination reflex. Early bladder training will promote his self-urination control. Your burden will become less. Let's try it, OK?

病人妻子:好的,我尽力试试。小姐,您有空吗?我想跟您单独谈谈。

Patient's wife: Fine, I'll try. Miss, I would like to talk to you in private if you have time.

护士:好吧,去我办公室吧。(病人妻子随护士进了办公室。)请坐。

Nurse: No problem, please come to my office. (The patient's wife

第二部分 外科护患沟通

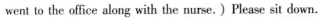

went to the office along with the nurse.) Please sit down.

病人妻子：谢谢（坐下，护士在其对面坐下，沉默片刻）。

Patient's wife: Thank you (sitting down, facing the nurse and keeping silent for a moment).

护士：梁太太，你很坚强，在病人面前你能做到像现在这样很不容易。我很愿意帮助你，无论是精神上或是对病人的护理上。

Nurse: Mrs. Liang, you are very brave. I'll help you whether it is psychological or how to take care of your husband.

病人妻子：谢谢！（沉默、流泪）我很矛盾，一想到今后我将面对一个瘫痪在床的丈夫一辈子，简直不知所措，我有自己的理想和事业，而现在……

Patient's wife: Thank you. (silent, sobbing). I'm in a dilemma and don't know what to do when I think that I'll have to face a paralyzed husband the rest of my life. I have my work and my dreams. But now...

护士：是的，任何人遇到如此巨大的灾难都将不知所措，然而我们毕竟还是要面对现实的。现在最关键的就是要支持和鼓励你丈夫，我们必须共同努力帮助他渡过术前、术中及术后的全部难关。手术效果越好，你所面对的难题也就愈少，而病人的各项功能也将恢复得越多、越好。我会始终在你身边，随时帮助你，支持你，相信我。

Nurse: Yes, everyone will be at a loss when facing such a situation like yours. However, we must face the reality. The most important thing you should do now is to support and encourage your husband. We should work together to help him go through all problems successfully before, during, and after the operation. The better the result of the operation, the fewer the problems you will have to face. I'm ready to help you at any time. Please trust me.

病人妻子：（紧紧握住护士的手，连声说）我相信你！

Patient's wife: (held the nurse's hand tightly and said) I believe you.

Part II　Surgical Nursing Care

结果 / *Result*

病人在医生、护士的鼓励下,在妻子的支持下顺利渡过了复位手术的全部难关。护士每天帮助和指导其做功能锻炼,妻子在旁积极配合。1个月后,病人已经坐在轮椅上,自己洗漱、进餐、自主排尿了。出院那天,夫妇俩向护士描绘了他们今后的生活计划,并希望她成为他们永远的朋友。

The patient successfully went through all the difficulties related to the reposition surgery with the encouragement of doctors and nurses and the support of his wife. The nurses helped and instructed the patient to do functional training every day and his wife cooperated with them. One month after the operation, the patient could sit in the wheelchair, brush his teeth, eat food and urinate by himself. On the day of his discharge from the hospital, they told the nurse-in-charge their plans for the future and hoped that she would become their permanent friend.

第二部分 外科护患沟通

多发性骨膜瘤病人的护理
Nursing Care for a Patient with Multiple Periosteoma

李惠玲

背景/ *Background*

病人王先生,男性,59岁,因多发性骨膜瘤而在两年内连续3次接受手术治疗。最近 CT 报告提示:又复发了,仍须手术而且可能要截肢。病人无法接受这样的事实。3次手术的痛苦以及术后的各种负担更使他失去活着的力量。尽管家属和医护人员一再瞒着不告诉他真实病况,然而,两年来躺在病榻上的痛苦历程使他彻底绝望了。病人要求回家,拒绝任何治疗。这时,护士该如何帮助他呢?

Patient Wang, male, 59 years old, had received three operations in the last two years because of multiple periosteoma. Recently, the computerized tomography (CT) showed recurrence. An operation must be performed and he may even need amputation. The patient couldn't face the reality. The three operations and the burdens after the operations had made him lose all the strength to live. Although his family members and the medical staff didn't tell him about all the facts, the bitter experiences of staying in bed had driven him despair completely. The patient wanted to

Part Ⅱ Surgical Nursing Care

go home and refused any treatment. How could the nurse help him?

交流 / Interactions

护士：老王，您想过没有，如果您放弃了治疗，任癌细胞肆意蔓延，您妻子、儿子他们会如何伤心吗？

Nurse: Mr. Wang, have you thought about how sad your wife and son would be if you give up treatment and let the cancer spread?

病人：正因为想到他们每次术后都要请假，日日夜夜守护我，陪伴我，所以我才更不该拖累他们。

Patient: It's because they had to take leaves after my previous operations and accompanied me day and night that I don't want to trouble them again.

护士：可是，您想过没有，他们是为爱和希望才这么做的。如果您放弃治疗，他们又如何能安心地工作和生活呢？他们将时刻惦记您的生命安危。一旦您离开了他们，他们能不悲痛欲绝，抱憾终身吗？请想想这些！

Nurse: But have you ever thought that they did this because of their love and hope for you. How could they work and live if you give up treatment? They will be worrying about you all the time. If you left them forever, how can they not feel sad and sorrowful all their lives? Please think about this!

病人：截肢意味着变成残废了，我无法接受这样的事实。

Patient: Amputation means that I'll become a crippled person. I cannot accept this fact.

护士：是的，失去一条腿，无论从肉体上还是心理上都将很痛苦。但是，想想这是为了保全生命，保持家庭的完整，只好忍痛接受这一残酷事实。何况还可以装假肢，如果恢复得好和原来相比不会有太多变化的。

Nurse: Yes, losing a leg is a bitter experience physically and mentally. But you must face this cruel reality in order to keep you alive and keep the integrity of your family. Besides, you may install an artificial leg after the operation. It won't be too much difference compared with before if you recover well.

病人：截肢后癌细胞还会再复发吗？

Patient: Is there any recurrence of the cancer after amputation?

护士：只要坚持化疗和放疗应该可以预防复发的。

Nurse: It can be prevented if you continue to have chemotherapy and radiation.

病人：看来也只好这样了。听您讲了这么多，我似乎又有了希望，谢谢您。

Patient: It seems that I really don't have any choice. After hearing what you've said, it seems that there is some hope for me. Thank you.

结果 / Result

病人经与护士的指导性交谈，逐渐走出了绝望心理，接受了截肢手术。

After the instructive talk with the nurse, the patient gradually came out of the psychological despair and received the amputation.

Part Ⅱ　Surgical Nursing Care

Ⅱ-5

车祸后病人的康复指导
Rehabilitation Instructions for a Patient in a Traffic Accident

沈梅芬　　徐颖

一次快乐的旅行因为司机的疏忽而演变为一场不可挽回的灾难。小沈同学不幸成为我们监护室的重症患者。然而,她又是幸运的,积极的抢救、坚强的意志力使她奇迹般迎来第2次生命,并以惊人的速度恢复着。拔除气管套管,搬出监护室,她异常兴奋。可是第2天,小沈一直闭眼沉睡,情绪低落,不愿说话。这对于生性活泼的小沈来说,极其反常。这时,床位护士来到了她身边,凑近她的耳朵,轻声呼唤。

A happy journey changed into a disaster because of the carelessness of the driver. Schoolgirl Shen unfortunately became our patient in the Intensive Care Unit (ICU). However, she is also fortunate because her life was miraculously saved due to excellent emergency rescue treatments and her own positive will power. She recovered very quickly. After the trachea tube was removed, she was moved out of the ICU. She expressed unusual excitement. However, the following day, Miss Shen did not open her eyes and slept all day. She was depressed and unwilling to talk. It was extremely abnormal for Miss Shen because of her usually optimistic nature. The nurse came to her bedside and whispered into her ear.

交流 / Interactions

护士:小沈,你恢复得很快,为什么不开心呢?

Nurse: Miss Shen, you are recovering so fast. Why are you unhappy?

(病人沉默,双眼继续合着。抖动的眼皮表明她已经听到了护士阿姨的话。)

(The patient kept silent, both her eyes still closed. The trembling upper eyelids indicated that she had heard the words of the nurse.)

护士:(继续轻声问)你能告诉我今天不开心的原因吗?或许阿姨能帮你解决问题。闷在心里不利于健康,更会影响你的恢复。

Nurse: (went on asking with a gentle voice) Can you tell me the reason why you are not happy today? Maybe I can help you solve the problem. Depression is not good for your health, and will affect your recovery.

(病人半信半疑地睁开眼。护士紧紧握了一下小沈的手,以传递更多的力量,给她树立信心。小沈示意爸爸拿来纸和笔,用颤抖的手虚弱地写下:"我是不是发生车祸了?我说话为什么不能发音?我的学习要跟不上了!")

(The patient opened her eyes. The nurse held her hands tightly to encourage her and to build up her confidence. Miss Shen signaled her father to bring the paper and the pen, and wrote down the following with her trembling hand, "Did I have a car accident? Why can't I say a word? I will fall behind on my school work.")

护士:是的,你是经历了一次车祸,但因为你的坚强,你的生命没

Part Ⅱ　Surgical Nursing Care

有受到丝毫影响。你说话不能发音是因为我们刚拔除了气管套管,只要你能克服因无声而拒绝说话的心理障碍,坚持每天说话,你会发现声音会一天比一天响亮。你是个聪明的孩子,所以学习更不用担心了。健康是学习的资本,有了健康的身体才能做更多的事情。所以现在的你要抛开一切顾虑,把身体养好,争取早日出院。

Nurse: Yes, you had a car accident. But because of your strong will, your life has not suffered too much. You cannot speak, because we just removed the trachea tube. Once you overcome the psychological barrier and stop refusing to talk, your voice will become louder day by day if you continue to practice talking. You are a smart girl. You don't need to worry about your studies. A healthy body is the foundation for study. You can do more things if you are healthy. Therefore, you'd better dispel any misgivings now, have a good rest, and try to be discharged from the hospital early.

病人:(咧开嘴笑了,丢下纸和笔,使劲说了声)谢谢!

Patient: (grinned, put down the paper and the pen, and managed to say) Thanks!

结果/ Result

两周后,小沈因全面迅速的恢复而出院了。临走时,所有医护人员都听到了她清脆响亮的告别声。

Two weeks later, Miss Shen had recovered enough and was discharged from the hospital. All the doctors and nurses heard her clear and loud voice saying, "Good-bye."

第二部分 外科护患沟通

点评 / Comments

在这段对话中,床位护士通过移情的交流变量,巧妙地运用了"沉默""接触"等非语言沟通技巧,确认病人的担心,给予其充分的鼓励和正向指导,帮助病人树立"新生"之信心。

In this episode, the nurse used non-verbal communication techniques such as "silence" and "touching" to identify with the patient's concern, to provide encouragement and positive guidance. It helped the patient regain her confidence to live, thus speeding up her recovery.

Part II Surgical Nursing Care

II-6

病人脊柱手术前的要求
A Patient's Request before a Spinal Surgery

宋良铮　王莉

背景 / Background

离休干部老童,战争年代脊柱负过伤。由于当时医疗条件差,手术效果很不理想。几十年过去了,老童早已从领导岗位上退了下来。脊柱也随着肌体的老化而最终形成了严重的侧弯。老童起先不愿手术治疗,他有两个担心:一是认为自己年岁已高,来日无多,再动手术纯属多余。二是担心手术中的风险变数,生怕自己躺上手术台就再也醒不了,好多事情还没向小辈交代。这天,老童被安排手术,他躺在手术床上,烦躁不安。手术室护士发现了这一切,她连忙走过去。

Mr. Tong, a retired official, had his spine wounded during the war. The operation on his spine at that time was unsatisfactory because of poor medical resources. Several decades have passed and Mr. Tong has retired from his leadership position. With aging his spinal column has become severely curved laterally. At first, Mr. Tong did not want to have surgical treatment. He was worried about two things: First, he thought that as an old man he would not live too much longer so why bother with the surgery.

第二部分 外科护患沟通

Second, he was worried about the risks of the surgery, fearing that he might die during the operation. There were a lot of things he had not yet handed over to his offspring. The day when he was scheduled for the surgery, Mr. Tong was lying on the operating table and felt very uneasy. The operating room nurse noticed this and walked to him immediately.

交流 / Interactions

护士:老同志,您怎么啦,需要我做什么吗?(由于事先对病人做过细致的了解,护士知道病人的身份,称其"同志"会使病人更觉亲切。)

Nurse: Comrade, are you feeling all right? Can I help you with anything? (Knowing much about the patient in advance, the nurse uses the term "comrade" hoping this may make him feel warm and closer.)

病人:没什么。(叹了口气)哎,我就觉得,人老了真没用,还在这里浪费国家的钱。

Patient: I'm fine. (sighing) I just feel I'm old and useless and wasting the country's money by staying here.

护士:(事先知道离休干部的医药开销均由国家财政承担,对老童这样说,从心底感到无比崇敬。)老同志,别这样说,您为国家的建立和建设都做出过巨大的贡献。现在国家经济形势好了,应该更加关注你们这些功臣的身体。我们也很愿意为您服务。

Nurse: (Knowing his medical expenses are paid by the government, the nurse is respectful to hear Mr. Tong's concern.) Comrade, please do not say that. You have made a great contribution to the establishment and construction of our country. Our national economic situation is much better now. It's our responsibility to take care of you and we are glad to do it.

病人:谢谢你,护士同志。我还有一个要求,不知……不知行不行。

Patient: Thank you, nurse. I just have one request. Could you help me?

护士:(看出老童有些为难)没关系的,您有什么要求尽管提。

Nurse: (noticing of hesitation on his face) No problem. Please

Part II Surgical Nursing Care

tell me.

病人：我是说，护士同志，我是说我这病挺严重的。我怕万一起不来……我想叫我儿子进来，我想见见他。

Patient: Nurse Comrade, you know my illness is very serious and I may die during the operation. I'd like to see my son. Could you ask him to come in?

护士：(明白老童是担心手术风险，对老童微微一笑)老同志，您提的要求照说也不过分。可是您知道吗，我们手术室是无菌环境，为了保障病人的健康，是绝对不能让除医务人员以外的人进入的。

Nurse: (Knowing he is worrying about the risks of the operation, the nurse smiles at the old man.) Comrade, your request is understandable. But do you know our operating room is aseptic? To safeguard the patient's health, no one else is allowed to enter the operating room except the medical personnel.

病人：(无奈，失望的表情)哦，是这样啊。

Patient: (helpless, disappointed) Ah, I see.

护士：(继续微笑着)同志，您就放心吧，像您这样的手术，虽说有一定的风险，可我们这里的医生、护士都多次承担过这样的手术，是有丰富的经验的。

Nurse: (smiling still) Comrade, don't worry. Although there may be some risks with your operation, our experienced doctors and nurses have successfully performed such operations many times.

病人：(表情开始舒展)好，我知道了。

Patient: (beginning to relax) OK, I understand.

护士：(趁热打铁)您现在要做的，就是抛开一切杂念，积极配合手术，争取早日康复。您和您儿子的话呀，还有很多年可以慢慢地讲呢！

Nurse: (grasping the opportunity) What you should do now is to concentrate on your operation, cooperate with us and concentrate on an early recovery. There will be many more years for you to talk with your son.

病人：(脸上露出笑容)是，是，我一定配合。

第二部分　外科护患沟通

Patient：(smiling) Yeah, I will do that.

结果 / Result

老童带着轻松、愉快的心态，积极配合手术。全身麻醉醒后，老童激动地握着护士的手，连声道谢。

With relaxed mood, Mr. Tong cooperated with the surgical procedure. After waking up from the general anesthesia, Mr. Tong held the nurse's hands firmly and thanked her repeatedly.

点评 / Comments

老童在等待手术时希望见儿子一面，这是对即将进行的手术恐惧、疑虑、担忧的表现，也是所有术前病人都存在的心理反应，是术前心理护理的重点。方法很多，需因人而异。老童是位久经沙场的离休干部，阅历较广，性格开朗，护士采用"联想"法引导他憧憬手术成功后的美好生活，以转移目前的紧张心理，从而安心、愉快地接受手术。方法得当，效果好。

The patient wanted to see his son while waiting for his operation. It is an indication of fear, misgiving, and worrying about the operation. It is also the psychological reaction that all preoperative patients have and it is the major part of preoperative psychological nursing care. Several methods can be used for providing the psychological care, and it varies from person to person. The patient is a retired cadre with many experiences and is broad-minded. The nurse used the "association" method to lead him to imagine the good life after a successful operation. She decreased the patient's nervousness and thus allowed the patient to accept his surgery with a more peaceful and happy mood. The method was proper and effective.

Part II Surgical Nursing Care

术中关爱
Care in the Operating Room

秦长喻　王莉

背景/ Background

一位 51 岁的女性膀胱肿瘤患者,在手术间等待手术。她过去的职业是会计。在等待时,病人将身体用棉被盖严实,并有吸鼻声。

A 51-year old female patient with a bladder tumor was waiting for surgery in the operating room. She worked as an accountant before she fell sick. While waiting, she covered herself with a cotton quilt and was making a sniffing sound.

交流/ Interactions

护士:您觉得冷吗?

Nurse: Are you cold?

病人:不冷。

Patient: No.

护士:你有鼻炎吗?需要加高枕头吗?

Nurse: Do you have a stuffy nose? Would you like me to raise the pillow higher?

第二部分 外科护患沟通

病人:谢谢,枕头倒不要,就是这儿有冷气吹到我鼻子里,我一吸到冷气鼻子就堵塞。

Patient: No, thanks. But I feel the cold air blowing on my face. I do have a stuffed-up nose from that.

护士:那我调高一点室温,好吗?

Nurse: Should I adjust the room temperature a little higher?

病人:谢谢。我不怕热,就怕冷。

Patient: Thanks a lot. I am not afraid of heat. A little higher temperature will be fine.

护士:不用谢,你有什么要求尽管跟我说。每个人对冷热的感受都不同,在这个房间以你的要求来调整,你不用客气。

Nurse: You are welcome. Just let me know whatever you want. Everyone prefers different temperatures. We will adjust it to your liking.

病人:这个风能不能不要对着我吹?

Patient: Could you adjust the fan so the breeze will not blow directly on me?

护士:可以。(在工人的协助下调整床的位置)这样可以吗?

Nurse: No problem. (adjusting the bed location with the worker's help) Is this better?

病人:谢谢,你们的态度真好,不影响什么吧?

Patient: Thanks. Your attitude is really good. I hope that I didn't bother you too much.

护士:不会影响什么的,手术时铺好消毒单你就吹不到风了,那时我们再把床移到正中,你放心。

Nurse: It's not a bother. You won't feel the breeze after they cover you with the aseptic sheet during the surgery. We will move the bed back then.

(患者很感激,有些过意不去,反复地谢着。)

(The patient was very grateful and also felt guilty about this request. She thanked the nurse repeatedly.)

Part II Surgical Nursing Care

护士:不用担心,床是多功能的,移动很方便。你有什么问题尽管跟我讲。

Nurse: Don't worry about it. This is a multi-functional bed which is very easy to move or change direction. Just tell me if you have any problems.

点评/ Comments

护患关系的本质是护理人员与护理对象之间的情感联系。手术室护士对于病人细微周到的关怀和主动帮助,表现了护理人员热忱的移情精神,能有效稳定病人的情绪,帮助他/她建立接受手术的最佳身心状态。

The essence of the nurse-patient relationship is the emotional contact between the nursing personnel and their clients. The sincere concern and active help given to the patient by the operating room nurses demonstrated the spirit and the empathy of these nurses. This effectively stabilized the patient's emotion, and helped to build his/her best mental and physical condition to face his/her surgery.

第二部分 外科护患沟通

乳房纤维瘤术前焦虑的疏导
Preoperative Guidance for an Anxious Patient with Breast Fibrosarcoma

方慧麟

背景/ Background

病人赵女士,50岁,政府干部。患乳房纤维瘤住院等待手术。入院后在同病室患乳房肿瘤已于术者的不良刺激下,茶饭不思,寝食难安,对自己将要进行的手术顾虑重重。吴护士适时地来到床边。

Patient Ms. Zhao, a 50- year old government official, was admitted to the hospital waiting for an operation for breast fibrosarcoma. The patients in the same ward who had already received their operations had influenced her negatively. She had no appetite and could not fall asleep. She was worried about her operation. Nurse Wu promptly came to her bedside.

交流/ Interactions

护士:赵阿姨,这几天您胃口不好,快开饭了,我给您服些开胃口的药吧(帮助服药)。过几天您要手术了,要多吃些有营养的食品才是啊。

Nurse: Ms. Zhao, you have no appetite these days. It's time to have

Part Ⅱ　Surgical Nursing Care

lunch. Let me give you a pill to stimulate your appetite (helping her take the pill). You'll have an operation in a few days. You should eat more nutritious food.

病人：我害怕极了。看着隔壁这位孙女士手术后,半个身体都被包扎起来了。开刀一定很痛,也不知效果怎么样!

Patient: I'm afraid of the operation. Look at Ms. Sun in the next bed. Half of her body is bandaged after the operation. It must be very painful and I don't know if her operation is a success.

护士：赵阿姨,乳房肿瘤是一种常见病、多发病,占女性肿瘤疾病的第二位。但只要早期诊断,早期治疗,是肿瘤疾病中预后最好、生存率最高的。手术后会有些疼痛,但这是暂时的,也是有办法解决的,康复才是最为重要的。

Nurse: Ms. Zhao, breast tumors are common. It is the second most frequent tumor among women. If diagnosed and treated early, it has the best prognosis and highest survival rate of all cancers. There will be some pain after the operation. But it will be temporary and can be eased with medication. The most important thing is a successful recovery.

病人：对面朱阿姨手术后都快出院了,可她的手臂还不能提起来,今后怎么办呢?

Patient: Ms. Zhu over there is going to be discharged from the hospital soon. But she still can't raise her arms. What will happen to her?

护士：饭菜来了,今天的菜多香啊!您一定要把这些饭菜都吃完啊。饭后休息一会儿,然后我来教您手术后手功能恢复的锻炼方法。朱阿姨出院后,经过几个月的功能锻炼后,她的手也会逐渐提起来的。

Nurse: Here comes your lunch. It smells delicious. You should try to eat all the food and then take a rest after lunch. I'll come back to teach you how to exercise your arms after the operation. Ms. Zhu will continue her exercises for a few months after she leaves the hospital and her hands will gradually be able to move.

病人：还有……(想再问问题)。

第二部分　外科护患沟通

Patient: And ... (wishing to ask again)

护士:我知道了,您是怕手术后由于体态的改变,会影响了您美丽的形象。

Nurse: I see. You're afraid that the change in your body will affect how you look like.

病人:是的。

Patient: Yes.

护士:这您放心。当代医学工程的成果已在临床上广泛应用。待您康复后,我们可以为您联系安装安全、可靠、轻便、耐用、仿真度高的人工乳房,一定会有助于您保持原有的好体型。快吃饭吧。

Nurse: Don't worry. The achievements of modern medical technology research have been applied extensively in the clinic. After you recover from the operation, we can arrange to have an artificial breast made for you. The procedure can be done safely and reliably, and the artificial breast will be light, durable, very convincing, and look real. It will help you keep your original figure. Please eat your lunch now.

病人:我比较不害怕了,我会试着多吃些的。我要真患上恶性肿瘤,手术后该怎么办呢?

Patient: Now I'm not as afraid as before for my surgery. I'll try to eat more. However, if the tumor is malignant, what should I do after the operation?

护士:肿瘤的性质一般要等病理切片以后才能真正确定。请您相信我们的医院和医生,一切会为您进行周密安排的。您目前的任务就是安心把身体调养到最佳状态,争取手术成功。饭凉了,快吃吧,午休后我再来同您聊聊,告诉您手术前后需要做的事情。

Nurse: The nature of the tumor will be determined by the pathologist. Please trust our hospital and doctors. We'll arrange a good plan for you. Your task is to take good care of yourself so that your body is in good condition. Do all you can to make the operation a successful one. Your lunch is getting cold. Eat your lunch now. After you've had a rest, I'll chat with

Part Ⅱ Surgical Nursing Care

you again and tell you what you should do before and after the operation.

病人：谢谢你，再见。

Patient：Thank you and see you later.

点评 / Comments

吴护士的这次术前健康教育比较理想。她先启发病人自己说出对手术的各种顾虑，然后再进行循循善诱的疏导，使病人确认了自己的顾虑是合乎情理的，是受到护理人员尊重的。在整个交谈的过程中，病人不感觉在被"教导"，而是护患双方在平等地讨论问题，从中及时、正确、充分地获得了有关手术问题的信息和知识，并感受到护士对她的同情、关怀和帮助，达到了消除病人顾虑、建立良好护患关系的预期目标。

The health education given to the patient before her operation was ideal. Nurse Wu encouraged the patient to reveal her worries. Then she systematically worked through them with the patient and offered guidance. She showed the patient that her worries were reasonable and were also respected. Throughout the communication, the patient did not feel that she was being "instructed", but that it was an equal discussion between nurse and patient. The information she received about the operation was timely, correct and complete. At the same time she received sympathy, care and support from the nurse. The goal of easing the patient's worries was achieved by creating a good relationship between the patient and the nurse.

第二部分 外科护患沟通

胃部术后舒适护理
Comforting a Patient after a Gastric Operation

毛莉芬

背景 / Background

病人李某做完胃部手术回到病房。3小时后麻醉完全清醒,床位护士来到病人身边。

Patient Li was sent back to the ward after stomach surgery. He woke up from the anesthesia 3 hours later. The nurse came to see him.

交流 / Interactions

护士:(看到病人的神情很痛苦,关切地问)老李,你哪儿不舒服,告诉我,好吗?

Nurse: (asking concernedly after seeing the patient looked painful) Mr. Li, can you tell me where you feel uncomfortable?

病人:我觉得全身不舒服。

Patient: My whole body is uncomfortable.

护士:是伤口疼痛吗?

Nurse: Is it the wound?

Part Ⅱ Surgical Nursing Care

病人：不是，我用了镇痛泵。我只是觉得浑身难受。

Patient: No. I'm using an analgesic pump now, but I still do not feel well.

护士：可能是在床上平卧的时间长了，让我来帮你换个体位，好吗？（护士协助病人翻成侧卧位，并妥善安排好腹腔引流管及胃肠减压管。）

Nurse: Maybe you've laid on your back too long. Let me help you to change your position. (The nurse assisted the patient to lie on his side, and arranged the abdominal cavity drainage tube and the gastrointestinal decompression tube to the proper position.)

病人：这么多管子在身上，我都不敢翻身。我真想拔掉这些管子，尤其是这根从鼻子插进去的胃管。

Patient: I dare not to turn my body with so many tubes in me. I really feel like pulling them out, especially the gastric tube through my nose.

护士：这么大的一个手术你都挺过来了，这些管子现在对你很重要，它们会帮你尽快恢复。不要怕，再坚持两天，我会尽力和你一起度过这个难关的。

Nurse: You've made it through the operation. These tubes are very important for you, because they can help you recover quickly. Don't be afraid. Persist for two more days. Let's overcome the barrier together.

病人：这些管子到底有什么作用，要多久才能拔掉呢？

Patient: What's the function of these tubes and when will they be removed?

护士：手术一般都会在腹腔内留下积液、积血。插在腹壁上的两根引流管主要是帮助引流腹腔中的积血或积液。2~3天后，引流液明显减少，医生就可以帮你拔掉两根管子了。至于胃管，是引流胃液用的，起初也有一些手术后的血液引流出来。你的胃部被切掉一部分，并和下面的肠子做了吻合，为了吻合口能愈合得更快、更好，胃本身分泌的胃液必须及时引流出来，否则会影响吻合口的愈合。过早拔掉管子，胃里液体太多，张力大了会让吻合的伤口裂开。

第二部分　外科护患沟通

Nurse: Usually there will be some blood and fluid accumulated in the abdominal cavity after the operation. The two drainage tubes placed in the abdominal wall are used to help drain the fluid. After two or three days, when the drainage fluid decreases, the doctor will take the tubes out for you. The gastric tube is used to drain the gastric fluid and some accumulated blood from your stomach. A portion of your stomach has been removed and the remaining portion was connected to the intestines below. In order to heal the wound better and more quickly, the gastric fluid must be drained out timely. If the tubes were taken out too early, the fluid would accumulate in the stomach, and the wound could split open due to the weight of the fluid.

病人：可是，胃管刺激我喉部的感觉，真难以忍受。

Patient: The gastric tube irritates my throat. It is really unbearable.

护士：你尝试着深吸气，再呼气，像我一样（示范深呼吸的动作），会好一些。还有，因为你的注意力都在这几根管子上，不舒服的感觉就会更明显了。

Nurse: Try to take a deep breath, then exhale, as I'm doing (giving a demonstration). It will make you feel better. You will feel more uncomfortable if you keep focusing and pay too much attention to these tubes.

病人：明天，我能让我的爱人把收音机带来听吗？

Patient: Could I ask my wife to bring a radio for me tomorrow?

护士：当然可以，我正想建议你这样做呢。你还可以做一些其他的事情，只要不经常想这些管子，就会感觉好多了。

Nurse: Of course, I am just about to suggest you do so. You can do other things as well. Just try not to think of the tubes too often.

病人：好的。这些管子既然那么重要，我会尽量克服的。谢谢你。

Patient: OK, I'll try to overcome the difficulties since they are so important to me. Thank you very much.

Part II Surgical Nursing Care

结果 / Result

在护士的指导和鼓励下,病人主动尝试转移注意力的各种方法。他让家人带来了收音机和他平时爱看的书籍,在疼痛不适可以忍受的情况下,听优美舒缓的音乐,看书,病人脸上的痛苦表情明显缓和。

With the nurse's guidance and encouragement, the patient tried many ways to divert his attention from the tubes and the discomfort. He asked his wife to bring him the radio and books he liked to read. By listening to nice music and reading books, the discomfort had become bearable. The painful expression in the patient's face had obviously eased.

点评 / Comments

护士对手术后病人的疼痛和不适有同理心,并进行针对性的指导,可以帮助病人发挥自身能动性,进行自我调节和自我护理,起到药物所不能达到的效果。

Providing proper guidance and sympathy toward the patients who are suffering from pain and discomfort after operations, the nurse can help them to bring out their initiative on self-adjustment and self-care to achieve even better outcome than solely depending on medicine.

第二部分 外科护患沟通

乳房术前担忧疏导
Counseling for an Anxious Patient before Breast Surgery

殷雪群　王莉

背景/ Background

刘小姐,23 岁,因患右乳纤维瘤,需在局麻下行纤维瘤切除术。患者因担心术中与术后疼痛,担心将来生育后的哺乳,以及肿瘤的性质和术后的复发问题,惶惶不安,来到手术室等待手术。

Miss. Liu, 23 years old, is suffering from fibroma in her right breast and is waiting for a fibromectomy under local anesthesia. She is worried about pain during and after the operation, concerned with whether the operation will affect her breastfeeding in the future, and the nature of the tumor and its recurrence possibility. She is very nervous in the waiting room.

交流/ Interactions

病人:手术会很疼吗?
Patient: Is the surgery very painful?
护士:手术时不会疼,但打麻药时有一点点,比做药敏实验好一

Part II Surgical Nursing Care

点,不用害怕。

Nurse: No, not during the surgery. There will be a little pain during the local anesthesia which is less painful than the skin allergy test.

病人:麻药的作用能维持多长时间?麻药过后会疼吗?

Patient: How long will the effect of the anesthesia last? Will I feel pain after the anesthesia wears off?

护士:一般麻药作用完全消失需2小时。手术中如果你感到疼痛,医师可随时适当添加麻药。术后如果疼痛得厉害的话,可根据医嘱服用止疼片。第二次服用止疼片应与前一次间隔6小时。

Nurse: Generally, the anesthetic will last for 2 hours. If you feel pain during the operation, the anesthetist will give you more anesthesia anytime. And if you feel pain after surgery, your doctor can prescribe pain medication for you. The time interval between the two pain medications is 6 hours.

病人:这手术会影响我将来喂奶吗?

Patient: Will this surgery affect my breastfeeding in the future?

护士:放心好了,一般不会有什么影响的。

Nurse: Don't worry. In general, it shouldn't.

病人:我的纤维瘤是良性的,还是恶性的?

Patient: Is my fibroid tumor benign or malignant?

护士:乳房纤维瘤一般为良性肿瘤。取出来的肿块我们将进行常规病理检查,报告在3个工作日后发出。到时你可以到外科门诊的候诊室取报告,有什么问题及时和医生取得联系。

Nurse: The mastofibroma is usually a benign tumor. A routine pathological examination will be done on the removed tumor, and the report will be available in three business days. You can pick up the report from the outpatient surgery clinic at that time. Don't hesitate to contact the doctor immediately if there is any problem.

病人:为我手术的医生是男是女?

Patient: Is the doctor who will operate on me male or female?

第二部分　外科护患沟通

护士：为你手术的是男医生。没关系的,不用害羞,手术时我们会一直陪在你身边。

Nurse：It's a male. But don't worry. We'll be at your side during the surgery.

病人：手术后我还会再生这样的瘤子吗?

Patient：Will the tumor recur after the surgery?

护士：一般不会,因为这与你体内的激素水平有关。你平时应少吃鸡肉等含有激素的食物。

Nurse：Usually it won't. The tumor is related to your body hormone level. You should eat less food such as chicken, which may contain artificial hormones.

(手术结束后。)

(After the surgery.)

护士：请你3天后来门诊让医生替你检查伤口的情况。一般7天拆线,术后可能出现的问题及怎样处理,在我刚才给你的健康处方上都有介绍,你回去看看。如有问题,可随时电话联系。祝你健康!

Nurse：Please come back to the outpatient clinic three days after discharge. The doctor will examine your incision wound. Generally, the stitches will be removed on the seventh day. What will happen and how to deal with the problems you may encounter after the surgery are all listed in the instructions I gave you. Please read them after going back home and contact us at any time if you have any problems. We hope you remain in good health.

点评 / Comments

疾病给病人带来了各种焦虑,手术又是一个较大的刺激,病人会产生更严重的心理反应。所以,他们在手术前存在的种种担忧是必然的,而这将会影响到手术的成败和术后的康复。因此,术前健康教育就显得分外重要。术前健康教育一般在决定手术时即已开始。大致包含饮食指导、活动和休息指导、心理健康指导、体检指导、术后康复

Part II Surgical Nursing Care

指导、家属指导、术前各方面的准备指导等内容。手术室护士对病人进行的行为指导是术前健康教育的重要组成部分。

  Illness will bring various anxieties to a patient, and the surgery itself is a bigger catalyst for serious psychological reactions. Anxieties they may have before their surgery are inevitable. Sometimes, these can affect the success of the surgery and their recovery from illness. Therefore, it is very important to give preoperative health instructions to patients. It should begin as soon as the decision to have surgery is made. Health education, in general, includes guidelines for nutrition, activity and resting, guidance for mental health and physical examinations, postoperative rehabilitation, instructions for family members, and preoperative preparations, etc. These guidelines are given by operating room nurses, and they are an important part of preoperative patient education.

第二部分 外科护患沟通

II-11

产妇入院指导
Admission Instructions for a Woman in Labor

吴山虹

背景/ Background

病房走廊里,一位孕妇从外面走来,床位护士迎了上去。

A pregnant woman comes into the hospital labor ward. A nurse walks up to greet her.

交流/ Interactions

护士:你好!你有什么需要协助的吗?

Nurse:Hi! Do you need any help?

病人:是的。我姓王。

Patient:Yes. My last name is Wang.

护士:很高兴见到你。我是李护士,你可以叫我小李。你有什么不舒服吗?

Nurse:Very nice to meet you. I am Nurse Li. You can call me Xiao Li. Do you have any discomfort?

病人:我怀孕已经39周,今天感到下腹有点胀痛,我想可能要生

Part Ⅱ Surgical Nursing Care

了,就来医院检查。围产期检查室的医生建议我住院,我就来了。

Patient: I am 39 weeks pregnant and feel a little distention pain in the lower abdomen today. I thought it may be time to give birth, so I came to the hospital to have it checked out. The doctor at the prenatal clinic suggested hospitalization, that's why I'm here.

护士:噢,别着急,我先带你到产房与助产士见面,并且做一些产科方面的检查。

Nurse: Oh, don't be nervous. I will take you to the delivery room to meet the midwife and have an obstetric examination.

病人:好的,谢谢你。

Patient: Good, thank you.

(李护士把王女士介绍给助产士后,暂时离开,王女士在产房做各项检查。40分钟后,助产士陪同王女士来到病房护士站。李护士边迎面打招呼边从助产士手中接过王女士的病历和检查单并快速看了一下。)

(After introducing Mrs. Wang to the midwife, Nurse Li left temporarily. Mrs. Wang had all the tests done. About 40 minutes later, the midwife accompanied Mrs. Wang to the nurses' station of the ward. Nurse Li greeted them, and received Mrs. Wang's medical record and test results from the midwife and reviewed them quickly.)

护士:从你的面部表情看来,检查结果很不错,不是吗? 床位都给你准备好了,我陪你过去。

Nurse: I can tell from your facial expression that the test results must be very good, aren't them? The bed is ready for you. I'll accompany you over there.

病人:太好了。

Patient: Great.

护士:这是你的床位。你现在感到累吗?

Nurse: This is your bed. Are you tired?

病人:有点累。

第二部分 外科护患沟通

Patient: A little.

护士:那就先躺下休息一会儿,我去通知营养室帮你准备午餐。十分钟后我再来给作入院介绍并了解一些你的情况,你看如何?

Nurse: Lie down and rest. I'll notify the nutrition department to prepare lunch for you. I will come back in 10 minutes and provide the admission introduction and also obtain some information from you, OK?

病人:好的。李护士,刚才助产士告诉我睡觉要采取左侧卧位,为什么?

Patient: Good. Nurse Li, the midwife told me to lie on my left side. Why?

护士:噢,取左侧卧位可增加子宫、胎盘之间的血流,对胎儿较为有利。

Nurse: Oh, lying on the left side can increase the blood flow between the uterus and the placenta. This is good for the fetus.

病人:原来如此,那我为了宝宝一定要坚持左侧卧位。(李护士协助产妇慢慢摆好了体位,盖上被子离开病房。)

Patient: I see. I'll lie on my left side for the sake of my baby. (Nurse Li helped the pregnant woman to lie down slowly, covered her with a quilt and left the room.)

(她回到办公室与营养科联系好了王女士的午餐,翻阅了王女士的门诊病历、围产期检查记录和刚才产房内做的检查结果,准备了体检用物、入院介绍单、孕妇保健手册来到王女士床旁,见产妇已起床,便问)

(Nurse Li returned to the nurses' station, contacted the nutrition department for Mrs. Wang's lunch, read her medical history, the prenatal record and the tests results. Then she prepared the guidelines for hospitalization, the introduction list and expectant mothers' healthcare manual, and then went to Mrs. Wang's room. Seeing that Mrs. Wang had already got up, she asked)

护士:王女士,休息了一会儿,现在感觉如何?

Part Ⅱ   Surgical Nursing Care

Nurse: Mrs. Wang, how do you feel after resting?

病人:好多了,谢谢。

Patient: Much better, thanks.

护士:现在我给你介绍一下医院的规章制度,好吗?

Nurse: I would like to introduce the hospital regulations to you now, OK?

病人:可以。

Patient: Sure.

(李护士把住院须知,作息、陪探等规章制度,病室内设施的应用,物品的存放,信号系统的使用方法,床位医师等一一作了介绍。)

(Nurse Li gave Mrs. Wang the introduction one by one, regarding the hospitalization, the regulation for activities, resting and visitation, the use of equipment in the ward, how to store personal belongings, the use of the signal system, and the doctors in charge of her bed, etc.)

护士:王女士,刚才给你介绍了这么多,能记住吗?

Nurse: Mrs. Wang, I told you so much information. Can you remember all of it?

病人:记住了,非常感谢你为我作了如此详细的介绍。

Patient: Yes, I can. Thank you very much for the detailed introduction.

护士:接下来我想帮你量个体温和血压。你喝过热水吗?

Nurse: I will measure your blood pressure and temperature now. Did you drink any hot water?

病人:没有。

Patient: No.

护士:好的,我们开始吧。

Nurse: Good, let's begin.

(李护士分别为王女士量了体温、脉搏、血压。告诉王女士测量的结果在正常范围,让她放心。)

(Nurse Li took Mrs. Wang's body temperature, pulse, blood pres-

第二部分 外科护患沟通

sure, and told her that the results were all normal so she would not be worried.)

护士:我还想了解一下你的一般情况。

Nurse: I'd also like to obtain some other information about you, OK?

病人:好的。

Patient: OK.

(在交谈的过程中,李护士针对产科护理评估单的内容,包括生活习惯、健康状况、食欲睡眠、大小便情况以及月经史、孕产史等逐一进行了评估。)

(During the conversation, Nurse Li carried out the assessment by following the obstetrics nursing assessment sheet that included life habits, health condition, appetite and sleeping pattern, menstruation history, and previous delivery history, etc.)

护士:王女士,从我了解的资料中看出你的身体很健康,分娩条件也较好,我想你一定能顺利度过分娩期的。目前你已经临近预产期,而且还有些下腹胀痛的感觉,需要住院观察,不要随便外出,好吗?

Nurse: Mrs. Wang, I can see from the data that you are healthy and your status for giving birth is good. I think that you can get through the birth smoothly. Since you are having some abdominal distention, you are near the delivery time now. You need to stay in the hospital for observation. So don't go out by yourself, OK?

病人:好的,可我很害怕分娩这一刻的到来。分娩的时候会很疼吗?

Patient: OK. But I am very afraid of giving birth. Giving birth can be very painful, right?

护士:一开始,子宫收缩、子宫颈扩张的时候会感到疼一点。应对疼痛的方法是首先自己要树立分娩信心,听从助产士的指导,阵痛间隙要充分休息以保持体力。如果你还是不能忍受疼痛的话,我们医院有一种镇痛分娩的方法,可以减轻你的疼痛。

Nurse: At the beginning, you will feel a little pain during uterine

Part Ⅱ　Surgical Nursing Care

contractions and cervix dilation. The methods to cope with the pain are building up confidence during your delivery, listening to the midwife's guidance, and resting in between the contractions to maintain your strength. If you still can't tolerate the pain, we can give you anesthesia to ease the pain.

病人：是吗？这种方法对宝宝会有影响吗？

Patient: Is that so? Will the anesthesia have any adverse effects on my baby?

护士：我们医院已经做过很多例数，一般情况下是没有影响的。在镇痛分娩的过程中，助产士会一直守候在你的身边，用监护仪对母亲、胎儿的情况进行持续监护。如发现异常，医生会及时采取措施的。

Nurse: Our hospital does this a lot. Generally speaking, there are no adverse effects. In the process of anesthesia, the midwife will stay at your bedside and monitor you and the baby's conditions. If something abnormal happens, the doctor will take care of it right away.

病人：噢，那等我先生来了，我们可以商量一下考虑用镇痛分娩。

Patient: Oh, when my husband comes here later, we will discuss the idea of using anesthesia.

护士：好的，等决定了告诉我，我会帮你与助产士联系的。小王，这几天你要多注意休息，加强营养，注意个人卫生，保持会阴清洁，勤换内裤，注意胎动变化。你会数胎动吗？

Nurse: Good. When you've made the decision, please tell me. I will help you contact the midwife. Mrs. Wang, you must have adequate rest, eat properly, be hygienic by keeping your vulva clean, change your underwear often, and note fetal movement. Do you know how to record fetal movement?

病人：会的，上次在孕妇学校培训时，陈老师已教过数胎动的方法：每天早、中、晚各数一小时胎动。每小时胎动不低于3次，说明胎儿情况良好。我说得对吗？

Patient: Yes, I do. Last time, at expectant mothers' training, Teach-

第二部分　外科护患沟通

er Chen taught us the method: record fetal movement for an hour every morning, noon, and evening. Each time there must be no less than 3 fetal movements, thus reflecting the fetus is in good condition. Right?

护士:非常正确。住院期间你要继续注意胎动,我们也会定时来听胎心音的。你如果感到下腹胀痛加重,或有见红、破水等情况应及时与我们联系。

Nurse: Right. You have to continue monitoring fetal movement while in the hospital. You should contact us right away if you feel your abdominal distension pain aggravated, see blood, or your water breaks.

病人:好的。太感谢你了。

Patient: Good. Thank you very much.

护士:我刚才给你说的事项在这2张单子上均有,如果你忘记的话,可以再看看。另外,你如果有什么问题可用信号灯呼我,我会马上过来。负责你床位的胡主任正在为另一位产妇做手术。等他回来我会及时通知他来看你,你放心休息吧。我过一会再来看你。

Nurse: What I've just explained to you is in these 2 sheets of paper. If you forget, you can review them again. In the meantime, if you have any problems, you can call me with the signal beacon. I will come right away. Doctor Hu, who is responsible for your delivery, is operating on another pregnant woman now. When she finishes, I'll ask her to see you. Rest now. I will see you again shortly.

病人:多谢你的介绍,使我很放心。再见!

Patient: Thanks for the introduction. I am not nervous anymore. Goodbye!

护士:再见!

Nurse: Bye!

Part Ⅱ　Surgical Nursing Care

Ⅱ-12

母乳喂养指导
Guidance on Breast Feeding

薛小玲

背景/ *Background*

刘女士马上就要分娩了。由于工作很忙,她想对孩子采取人工喂养,但听朋友说,母乳喂养对母子都比较好。她不知道,这该怎么办?这天,她特意来到医院向产科护士请教。

Ms. Liu will soon give birth to a baby. Because of her busy work schedule, she is considering feeding the baby with formula. However, she has heard from her friends that breast-feeding is better for the baby and the mother. So what should she do? To help her decide, she went to the hospital and asked an obstetric nurse.

交流/ *Interactions*

刘女士:我怀孕了,快要做妈妈啦。请问母乳喂养究竟有哪些好处?

Ms. Liu: I am pregnant and will be a mother soon. Could you please tell me some of the advantages of breast-feeding?

护士:你一定愿意你的宝宝生长发育得很好,是不是?那么婴儿

第二部分　外科护患沟通

最理想的天然营养品就是母乳。因为它既经济简便又温度适宜,同时还能提高免疫功能,增强抗病能力,促进脑细胞的发育。对你来说还可以促进子宫复原,减少产后出血,降低乳癌、卵巢癌的发病率,并且还可以增进母子感情。

Nurse: I'm sure you want your baby to grow well. The best natural nutrition for an infant is the mother's milk. Because it is not only economical, simple and the proper temperature, but it can also strengthen the baby's immune system, increase the baby's anti-disease capability, and promote the growth of the baby's brain cells. At the same time, it can also help your uterus recover, reduce postpartum bleeding, and reduce the chances of breast and ovarian cancer, while promoting bonding between you and your baby.

刘女士:母乳喂养有这么多好处,我决定自己喂哺宝宝。但纯母乳喂养,这又是怎么一回事?

Ms. Liu: With so many advantages, I have decided to breast feed my baby. But what is "pure breast feeding"?

护士:噢!就是母亲用自己的奶喂自己的孩子,不给孩子吃任何液体或固体食品,也不用其他母亲的奶喂自己的孩子。

Nurse: Oh, "pure breast feeding" means you feed your baby with nothing but your own breast milk. No other liquids or solid food, nor other woman's breast milk.

刘女士:什么时候应该用纯母乳喂养呢?

Ms. Liu: When should the baby be fed with pure breast milk?

护士:在产后4~6个月内要求用纯母乳喂养,因为这个时期最适合婴儿营养需要、促进婴儿生长,母乳是最理想的食品。

Nurse: During the first 4 to 6 months after birth when the baby needs the most nutrition for growth.

刘女士:我再问一下,是否产后都要母婴同室呢?

Ms. Liu: I have another question. Should the mother and her infant stay in the same room after birth?

Part II Surgical Nursing Care

护士:是的。母婴同室就是指母婴同住在 1 个房间内,24 小时都是这样。医疗或给孩子护理的操作时,母婴分离不超过 1 小时。

Nurse: Yes. The mother and her infant stay in the same room for 24 hours a day with no more than one hour of separation for medication or nursing of the infant.

刘女士:为什么必须执行母婴同室呢?我真想知道得更多一些。

Ms. Liu: Why? I want to know more.

护士:这是为了能促进乳汁分泌,保证足够的乳汁,保证按需哺乳,还能增进母婴感情。

Nurse: Because it will increase the mother's milk production, ensuring enough milk for the infant, and it helps promote mother-infant bonding.

刘女士:所谓"早吸吮"又是怎么一回事?

Ms. Liu: What is "early sucking"?

护士:"早吸吮"是指产后半小时内母婴皮肤接触和协助哺乳,时间不得少于 30 分钟。但要母亲舒适,婴儿有准备,并且要在有吃奶的表示时,开始喂奶。就是婴儿有觅食反射、吸吮动作等。

Nurse: "Early sucking" means mother-infant skin contact and assisted breast-feeding within half an hour after birth. This should last no less than 30 minutes. However, breast-feeding can only begin when the mother feels comfortable and the baby shows signs of sucking or mouth reflex movement.

刘女士:"早吸吮"对婴儿又有哪些好处呢?

Ms. Liu: What is the benefit of "early sucking"?

护士:及早吸吮能刺激泌乳反射,增加乳汁分泌。尤其是初乳可以增加婴儿抗病能力;促进婴儿肠蠕动,早排胎粪;减少、减轻新生儿黄疸的发生;增加产妇子宫收缩,预防产后出血。

Nurse: "Early sucking" stimulates reflexes and increases milk-production. The first milk increases the infant's anti-disease ability, promotes peristalsis and passing of fetal stool, reduces infant jaundice, increases the mother's uterine contractions and prevents postpartum hemorrhage.

刘女士:"按需哺乳"的目的和意义又是什么?

Ms. Liu: What is the purpose and meaning of "feeding on demand"?

护士:"按需哺乳"就是按照新生儿的需要哺乳,不限次数和时间。如果母亲感到奶胀不舒服,就可以让婴儿吃奶。

Nurse: "Feeding on demand" is to feed the infant when needed without restriction on the frequency and has no fixed time. For example, when the mother feels breast distension, she can feed her infant.

刘女士:是否每一个产妇都要实行按需哺乳呢?

Ms. Liu: Should all mothers practice "feeding on demand"?

护士:是的。因为按需哺乳能促进乳汁分泌,保证足够的乳汁,增进母婴感情,预防母亲奶胀。那又何乐而不为呢?

Nurse: Yes. Because it can help the mother's milk flow, help to promote bonding between the mother and her baby, and prevent the mother's breast distension. So why not do it?

刘女士:我很想知道母亲正确的哺乳姿势有哪几种?

Ms. Liu: I would like to know what the correct postures for breast-feeding are?

护士:哺乳有3种体位,就是坐势、卧势(仰卧、侧卧)和环抱式。

Nurse: There are three postures, sitting, lying (on your back, or side) and holding the baby.

刘女士:哺乳应怎样做呢?

Ms. Liu: How should the mother breast feed the baby?

护士:最好是母亲放松、舒适,婴儿身体贴近母亲,脸向着乳房,鼻子对着乳头,头与身体成一直线(胸贴胸、腹贴腹、下颌碰到乳房),母亲手托着婴儿的臀部。

Nurse: The best way is for the mother to sit down and relax, and put the baby's face close to her breast. Position the baby's nose next to her nipple, allowing bodies to form a straight line (chest to chest, belly to belly, chin to the breast), while the mother's hand holds the baby's buttocks.

Part Ⅱ Surgical Nursing Care

刘女士:怎样让婴儿正确地含接乳头,吸吮奶水呢?

Ms. Liu: How can I help the baby suck the milk correctly?

护士:你可以用乳头轻轻碰碰婴儿的上嘴唇,诱发觅食反射。婴儿张大嘴吸入乳头及大部分乳晕,慢而深地吸吮,有时会有暂停,能看见吞咽动作和听见吞咽声音。

Nurse: You can touch the baby's upper lip with your nipple, which will induce the baby's desire for sucking. Let the baby's mouth cover your nipple and most of your areola. Allow the baby to suck the milk slowly and deeply, pausing from time to time to allow the baby to swallow the milk.

刘女士:在喂奶时应该怎样正确地托好乳房?

Ms. Liu: How should I hold my breast when feeding?

护士:你把食指到小指四指并拢贴在乳房下的胸壁上,用食指托乳房的底部,拇指轻轻放在乳房上方,母亲的手不应离乳头太近。

Nurse: Put your four fingers together on your chest just bellow the breast and place your forefinger on the bottom and your thumb on the upper part of your breast. The mother's hand should not be too close to the nipple.

刘女士:假如我有事外出或奶太胀时应该怎样进行挤奶?

Ms. Liu: What is the proper way to express the milk when I'm not at home or feel breast distention?

护士:挤奶有几点要注意:1. 母亲的手必须彻底洗净。2. 坐立均可,要自己感到舒适,再将容器靠近乳房。3. 大拇指放在乳头根部上2 cm的乳晕上,食指放在拇指对侧之乳晕上,其他手指托着乳房。用拇指与食指的内侧向胸壁方向轻轻压挤,手指要固定,不要在皮肤上移动,重复挤压—松弛达3~5分钟。沿乳头依次挤压所有乳窦。

Nurse: When expressing milk you should: (1) Wash your hands. (2) Assume a comfortable position, either sitting or standing, then place a container near your breast. (3) Place your thumb on the areola 2cm above the nipple, and your forefinger on the areola opposite the thumb. Use your other fingers to hold your breast. Using the inner part of your

第二部分　外科护患沟通

forefinger and your thumb, press your breast tissue around the nipple gently towards the chest wall for 3 to 5 minutes to squeeze the milk out. Do not move the fingers on the skin.

刘女士：我又怎样知道我的奶够不够孩子的需要？

Ms. Liu：How do I know whether my milk is enough for my baby?

护士：这个问题问得好。我告诉你以下6点你就知道了：1. 每天喂奶次数要达8次以上。2. 母亲有乳胀的感觉。3. 喂奶时听见吞咽声。4. 每天可换下婴儿6块或更多的湿尿布。5. 婴儿体重增加平均18~30克/日或125~210克/周。6. 两次喂奶期间婴儿安静。

Nurse：This is a good question. You need to：(1) Nurse the baby at least 8 times a day. (2) Have a feeling of breast fullness. (3) Listen for swallowing sounds while feeding. (4) Change 6 or more diapers for baby every day. (5) The baby's weight should increase on average by 18 to 30g per day or 125 to 210g per week. (6) Baby is quiet between feedings.

刘女士：我担心乳汁不够，怎样可以保证有足够的母乳呢？

Ms. Liu：I am afraid that I may not produce enough milk. How can I make sure I'll have enough milk for my baby?

护士：这的确是母亲应该关心的问题。要做到充分有效的母乳喂养，就要做到早吸吮，按需哺乳，喂奶姿势正确，鼓励和支持母亲树立信心，保持愉快情绪，合理营养和休息，不给婴儿过早添加辅食。

Nurse：Many young mothers have the same concern. Effective breast feeding requires early sucking, feeding on demand, correct posture, confidence in your ability, a pleasant mood, sufficient nutrition and enough rest. Additionally, don't give the baby other food too early.

刘女士：假如乳房肿胀，最常见的原因是什么？

Ms. Liu：What are the common reasons for breast distention?

护士：主要是生产后最初几天没有做到充分有效的母乳喂养（未按需哺乳）或姿势不正确。

Nurse：The main reason for this is ineffective breast feeding (not feeding when needed) or incorrect posture.

Part Ⅱ Surgical Nursing Care

刘女士:假如乳头疼痛,又是什么原因?应该怎样处理?

Ms. Liu: What causes nipple pain and how can I deal with it?

护士:乳头疼痛主要是婴儿含接姿势不正确,没有将乳头乳晕放在婴儿的嘴里。处理的方法就是掌握正确的含接姿势,要将乳头及大部分乳晕含入婴儿口中。坚持频繁哺乳,每次哺乳结束时,挤出少量乳汁涂在乳头和乳晕上,短暂暴露,使之干燥。此外还要穿戴棉制的宽松内衣及胸罩。母亲不要用酒精或肥皂擦洗乳头。

Nurse: Nipple pain is caused when the baby doesn't hold the nipple and areola in the mouth correctly. To prevent nipple pain, you should make sure the baby is sucking the nipple correctly and you should also feed the baby more frequently. Each time you finish feeding the baby, press a little milk out, spreading it on your nipple and areola, and wait until it dries. You should also wear loose cotton underwear and bras. Don't wash your nipple with alcohol or soap.

刘女士:你能否告诉我,母亲患哪些疾病不能给孩子喂奶?

Ms. Liu: Can you tell me which diseases prevent a mother from breast-feeding?

护士:母亲如果患心脏病、肾脏病、精神病、癫痫、甲肝急性期伴有黄疸时;或母亲在哺乳期使用禁止的药物,如放射性药物,抗甲状腺药物时,是不宜给孩子喂奶。

Nurse: A mother can't breast feed her baby if she has heart disease, kidney disease, mental illness, epilepsy, acute hepatitis with jaundice, or if she is taking medication such as radiation treatment or anti-hyperthyroid medication.

刘女士:谢谢你!今天我从你那儿学到很多哺乳方面的新知识,我一定要牢记,并且照做,因为这是对孩子的生长和我们做母亲的都有益的。

Ms. Liu: Thank you very much. I've learned a lot about breast-feeding. It's very useful and will benefit both me and my baby. I'll follow your advice. Thanks.

第二部分　外科护患沟通

点评/ Comments

母乳喂养是自然界赋予人类的本能喂养方法。在免疫、营养、生理及心理方面有着特殊的功能,对母亲和婴儿都有诸多益处。在上述对话中,护士向准妈妈(刘女士)详细介绍了与母乳喂养相关的一系列问题及其实施过程中的注意点,使她在分娩前充分认识到母乳喂养的好处和重要性,为分娩后正确的母乳喂养奠定基础。

Breast feeding is one of the appetence of human beings. It has some special functions in immunity, nutrition, physiology and psychology, so it is beneficial to both infant and mother. In this episode, the nurse presented the related issues concerning breast feeding in detail, and let the soon-to-be new mother know the benefits and importance of breast feeding. So she developed a solid foundation for her to breast feed her baby correctly after the baby is born.

Part Ⅱ　Surgical Nursing Care

视网膜脱离病人的术前指导
Preoperative Instructions for a Patient with Retinal Detachment

王洁

背景/ Background

患者倪先生,25岁,因左眼视网膜脱离而住院准备手术治疗。患者有近视(左眼600度、右眼500度),在某合资企业任职,平时喜爱运动。发病前与同事一起踢了一场足球。现准备行左眼玻璃体切割术。床位护士小张来到病人床边。

Patient Mr. Ni, 25 years old, was admitted to the hospital for an operation to repair the retinal detachment in his left eye. He has myopia (left eye 600°, and right eye 500°). He works in a joint-venture enterprise. He likes sports. After playing soccer with his colleagues, his retina in the left eye was detached. He would have vitrectomy of that eye the next morning. Miss Zhang, the nurse on duty, came to talk to him.

交流/ Interactions

护士:小倪,您好! 明天就要做手术,现在我要为你做术前准备,并告诉你手术后的一些注意事项。

第二部分　外科护患沟通

Nurse: Good morning, Mr. Ni. The operation will be tomorrow. I will go over a few things with you to prepare for the operation and to tell you what you need to know after the operation.

病人:哦,好的,谢谢你。今天早晨查房时医生已告诉我手术的方法,而且说手术有一定的难度和风险,所以我很担心手术后的效果。

Patient: Oh, that's fine. Thank you. The doctor told me about the procedures of the surgery when making his round this morning. He said the operation would have certain difficulties and risks, so I'm worried about the operation.

护士:医生和你讲清楚手术的难度和风险是对的。这种手术比较复杂,手术时间也较长,开展这种手术的医院也不是很多。但是你放心,我们科开展这种手术已有一段时间,手术做得较多,效果也不错,只是手术的成败与你密切相关。

Nurse: It's the doctor's duty to inform you of the difficulties and risks of this operation. Although the operation is more complicated and may last a little longer, and only a few hospitals perform it, you don't have to worry. Our department has been doing this operation for some time. A lot of patients have had the operation and the results were very good. However, it is intently interrelated to you whether the operation will be successful or not.

病人:噢,那我该怎么做呢?

Patient: Oh, what should I do?

护士:手术的时候在你的眼睛里要打一种特殊的油,这种油打了以后使你的视网膜能够复位。手术后要采取俯卧位或低头坐位持续两周,一直保持这样的位置是很累的,所以,你现在可以先试着感受一下,有一个适应的过程。

Nurse: The doctor will inject a special kind of oil into your eye during the operation. This will reduce your retina problem. You should maintain a "prone position" or the "lowering your head sit-up position" for about two weeks after the operation. It will be very tiring to keep this position

Part Ⅱ Surgical Nursing Care

continually. So you may want to practice now to get used to it.

病人：平时我习惯侧睡，现在要我趴在床上睡两个星期真的很难受的。我可以先试着练练，想到这是为了视力早点恢复，我会尽力适应的。

Patient：I used to sleep on my side. It will be hard for me to sleep in a prone position for two weeks. But I'll try it because it's important to my early vision recovery. I will do my best.

护士：真是好样的，我们会尽量帮助你的。另外，术后你要多吃粗纤维的蔬菜和水果，少量多次饮水，保持大便通畅，不能用力摒。

Nurse：Good man. We will assist you to the best of our ability. In addition, you need to eat more vegetables and fruit that have coarse fibers, drink more water but small amounts each time, maintain free bowel movements, and don't push too hard when you go.

病人：哦，这也有关系呀。

Patient：Oh, are these all related to the recovery too?

护士：关系大着呢。术后你脱下的网膜正慢慢恢复，被你大便时用力一摒，网膜就会再次脱落，那样手术就白做了。

Nurse：Yes, it's very important. After the operation, your detached retina recovers slowly. However, if you push too hard while having a bowel movement, the retina may become detached again. Then the operation will be in vain.

病人：原来是这样。那还有要注意的吗？

Patient：Oh, I see. Are there any other things I need to pay attention to?

护士：手术后尽量少讲话，也不要大笑。另外出院后，半年内也不能运动或做重体力劳动，更不能踢足球，所以你的足球瘾要戒了。

Nurse：After the operation, you should speak as little as possible and don't laugh too hard. In addition, you can't participate in any sports or heavy physical labor. So you'll have to give up playing your favorite soccer game for a while.

第二部分　外科护患沟通

病人：看来为了眼睛我只能忍痛割爱了。听你这么一讲,我知道手术后应该怎么做了。

Patient: It seems that I must stop doing many of the things I love to do for my eye. I know now what I need to do after the operation. Thanks for your instructions.

护士：那好吧,我现在要帮你剪睫毛了,再有什么问题可找我。

Nurse: OK. Now I will help you trim your eyelashes. If you have any questions, please ask me at any time.

点评 / Comments

视网膜脱离患者手术后的卧位、饮食关系到病人术眼的恢复。张护士在利用给病人做术前准备的时机,耐心细致地告知其手术方案以及如何配合的方法,使病人对手术和康复有充分的准备。

The recovery and prognosis of the patient's eye are related to the sleeping position and the patient's diet after the retinal detachment operation. Nurse Zhang used the opportunity while preparing the patient for his operation to tell him the procedures of the operation, and how to cooperate with the staff. All these allowed the patient to be prepared for the surgery and its recovery.

Part Ⅱ　Surgical Nursing Care

巨大脑膜瘤术后饮食指导
Dietary Instructions after a Large Meningioma Surgery

王婷　朱巍巍　程平

 背景/ *Background*

患者朱先生,男性,35 岁,因巨大脑膜瘤收住院行手术治疗。手术后第3 天,患者主诉头晕目眩,恶心呕吐,精神萎靡。护士小张清晨来到病房。

Patient Mr. Zhu, 35 years old, was admitted to the hospital and received surgical treatment because of a large Meningioma. The third day after the operation, he complained of dizziness, nausea and vomiting, and weakness. Nurse Zhang came to talk to him in the morning.

交流/ *Interactions*

情境一/Scene 1
护士:朱先生,今天早饭吃了吗?
Nurse: Mr. Zhu, have you had your breakfast yet?
病人:(轻轻地摇了摇头)
Patient: (shaking his head slightly)

第二部分　外科护患沟通

护士：怎么啦，哪儿不舒服？
Nurse: What happened? What's wrong with you?

病人：感觉不太好，胃也不舒服，一吃东西就吐，刚才喝了一点米汤，又吐了。
Patient: I feel awful. My stomach feels sick too. I feel like vomiting immediately after eating. And I just vomited right after I drank some rice soup.

护士：哦，您的胃原来有过什么问题吗？
Nurse: Really? Did you have any problems with your stomach before?

病人：是的，有慢性胃炎。
Patient: Yes. I have chronic gastritis.

护士：这样啊，您不要担心。这两天您刚手术完，由于上全身麻醉，对胃肠功能会有一定的影响，加上您原来的胃不太好，恢复可能比别人相对要慢一些，而且您一直没吃进去多少东西，空腹时，胃酸也会刺激胃黏膜引起不适。另外您的头部手术其实是个相当大的手术，手术前您不是也知道肿瘤长得很大，现在手术后有一个脑子处于水肿期，这时也会出现呕吐现象的，但这些现在都可以通过药物来控制和改善。您等会试着在我帮您挂上甘露醇后再进食，看看会不会比现在好些，不要紧张，因为紧张情绪也会导致呕吐的。待会您先喝点温热的开水，再喝些米汤，因为米汤对胃黏膜是有保护作用的。

Nurse: I see. But take it easy. Your operation was only 2 days ago. Usually the general anesthesia will affect the gastrointestinal function and, on top of that, you've had stomach problems before, so it may take longer for you to recover. Because you've not been eating much, your stomach is almost empty. The gastric acid can stimulate the gastrointestinal membrane and cause an upset stomach when empty. Furthermore, the surgery you underwent was a complex one because you had a large tumor. After the doctors removed it, there is a period of brain edema. During this period you might vomit as well. But your upset stomach can be controlled and minimized by the medication. Please try to take some food again after the IV is finished transfusing. Then let's see whether the situation improves. Meanwhile, try not to be too nervous because nervousness can also cause

Part Ⅱ　Surgical Nursing Care

vomiting. Drink some warm water before you have the rice soup. The latter can help to protect your gastric membrane.

病人：是吗,现在这样的问题可以改善吗?

Patient：Really? Do you think it will improve the situation?

护士：会的,医生马上就要来查房了,对于您胃的问题,今天我一定会建议他们帮你仔细斟酌,对症下药。可是您要明白手术后的营养问题很重要,它会直接影响到您的恢复情况。如果您一直不吃东西,非但不利于胃肠功能的恢复,还会导致抵抗力下降,伤口愈合不佳,也会增加感染的机会,那会使您的疾病预后很慢,增加您的痛苦,增加您的住院费用,也增加了家人的负担。所以,目前我们要共同努力的是解决吃饭问题。

Nurse：Sure. The doctors will come to see you soon for their morning ward round. I will suggest they should prescribe some medicine to alleviate your stomach problem. But you must realize that nutrition after the operation plays a very important role. It will directly influence your recovery time. If you don't eat anything, it will not only delay the recovery of the gastrointestinal function but also lower your immunity. Imperfect healing of the incision will enhance the possibility of infection which will impact the prognosis and you might feel more pain. It will also increase the costs of your hospital stay, and bring much more burden to your family. Therefore, the most important thing we should do now is to solve your diet problem.

病人：是啊,可我的胃会很快好起来吗?

Patient：I agree with you. But will my stomach recover soon?

护士：会的,现在医学这么发达,新的药物越来越多,治疗胃病的药有很多都很有成效。您现在开始还要注意每天饮食的规律性,要少量多餐,这两天都吃些汤类和软烂消化的东西,比如米汤和牛奶,不过牛奶也要适量,可以让家里炖鸡蛋、烧些黑鱼汤等等。进食时可以把床头摇高些。建立自主胃肠道饮食要比静脉输液更重要,有很多营养是输液所不能补给的,必须要靠您自己吃下去,懂吗?

Nurse：Yes. Medical science has advanced so much and a lot of new medications have been developed. We have plenty of drugs which have

第二部分 外科护患沟通

been proven to be very effective to treat stomach problems like yours. In addition to medication, you still have to maintain your regularity of food intake. We suggest you take small amounts of food several times a day. In the next two days you can have some liquid and a light diet such as rice soup and fresh milk, just an appropriate amount of milk, not too much. You can also ask your family to cook some stewed eggs or millet soup for you. Keep your bed raised when you eat. It's much better to eat food rather than receive transfusions. There are a lot of nutrients that liquid transfusions cannot provide, and you have to eat the food by yourself. Do you understand?

病人：好的，我明白了，谢谢你。

Patient: Yes. I understand. Thanks a lot.

护士：不客气，我去帮您准备输液，等会再来看您。

Nurse: You are welcome. Now I am going to prepare the transfusion for you. I'll be back soon.

情境二/Scene 2

（护士小张帮病人挂上了甘露醇，并根据医嘱静脉推注了洛塞克，而后再次来到病人床边。）

(Nurse Zhang transfused the Sodium Glutamate and injected Ranitidine for Mr. Zhu. Then she came back to the patient again.)

病人：我刚才吃了一小碗稀饭和肉松，是不是像你说的甘露醇的作用，我没吐。

Patient: I have just eaten some dried shredded meat and a small bowl of porridge. The IV worked as you had mentioned, and I didn't throw up.

护士：哦，是吗？真是太好了，您看关键还是您自己的配合，情绪放松了就不吐了，继续努力好吗？

Nurse: Oh, really? That's great! You can see how important your cooperation is. When you relax, the sickness goes away. Please keep it up.

病人：好的，谢谢你。

Patient: I will. Thanks.

护士：没关系，您如果有什么问题马上叫我，我过一会再来看您。

Part II　Surgical Nursing Care

Nurse：You are welcome. Please call me if you have any problems. I'll be back later.

（病人灿烂地笑着点点头。）

(The patient nodded his head with a splendid smile)

结果 / Result

朱先生和床位护士小张建立了良好的护患关系。在小张的优势照顾下，朱先生很快顺利度过脑水肿期，克服了原有的胃部不适，半个月后康复出院。

A good patient-nurse relationship was established between Mr. Zhu and Nurse Zhang. Mr. Zhu went through the brain edema period smoothly under Nurse Zhang's skillful care. He also overcame his upset stomach and went home after 15 days.

点评 / Comments

手术后的饮食营养问题一直是病人所缺乏的疾病康复知识。护士必须时时刻刻注意给予病人有效的饮食指导，从而也能建立更好的护患关系，使健康教育更有收效。

Patients usually lack knowledge related to diet and nutrition after their surgeries. So nurses should give them effective diet instructions all the time. This also helps to establish a good relationship between the patient and the nurse, and makes the health education more successful.

第二部分 外科护患沟通

心脏移植病人的心理护理
Psychological Nursing Care for a Heart Transplant Patient

王玉宇

背景 / Background

患者朱女士,28岁,高中学历。因扩张性心肌病晚期施行了心脏移植手术。手术后收住监护室,特别护理。

Patient Ms. Zhu, 28 years old, a senior high school graduate, received a heart transplant because of dilated cardiomyopathy. After the operation, she was sent to the intensive care unit for special nursing care.

交流 / Interactions

情境一/Scene 1

术后当晚,经过4小时麻醉苏醒期,病人清醒。由于气管插管接人工呼吸机辅助呼吸,无法说话,只能用点头等简单的动作来表示她的意思。护士很清楚这时病人的心理情况,一直陪伴在身边。

Four hours after the operation, the patient regained her consciousness from the anesthesia. She couldn't talk because a tracheal tube was con-

Part Ⅱ　Surgical Nursing Care

nected to the respirator. She could only express herself with some simple actions, such as nodding, etc. The nurse knew Ms. Zhu's psychological situation, so she stayed with her.

护士:(轻轻握住病人的手,语气轻柔)朱女士,你能听到我在喊你吗?

Nurse: (holding the patient's hand and talking to her softly) Ms. Zhu, can you hear me?

病人:(轻轻点点头,闭着眼睛)

Patient: (nodding slightly with her eyes closed)

护士:你醒了?感觉还好吗?知道吗,你已经动完手术了,很成功。现在已经在病房了。我是小李,记得我吗?

Nurse: You are awaken. How do you feel now? The operation was a success and you are in the ward. I am Nurse Li. Do you remember me?

病人:(点点头)

Patient: (nodding her head)

护士:好的。朱女士,听我讲,你的移植手术做得非常成功。现在为了减轻你的负担,要用呼吸机帮助你呼吸一段时间,所以插在嘴里的管子还不能拔掉,有点难受,忍一忍,好吗?你只需好好地跟着机器呼吸就行了。我们给你用了镇痛剂,暂时不会觉得疼痛,好好休息,我会一直在边上陪你的。

Nurse: OK. Ms. Zhu, congratulations. Your operation was very successful. The respirator will help you to breathe for some time. Therefore the tube in your mouth cannot be taken out. You may feel discomfort but you must endure it during this short period. You should follow the rhythm of the respirator to breathe. We have given you some analgesic so you won't feel pain. Now take a good rest and I will stay with you.

(病人点点头,握紧护士的手。)

(The patient nodded her head, grasped the nurse's hand firmly.)

护士:别怕,我不离开,你放心睡吧。

第二部分　外科护患沟通

Nurse：Don't worry. I won't leave. Relax and sleep now.

（病人握着护士的手睡着了。）

（The patient fell asleep while holding the nurse's hand.）

情境二/Scene 2

（术后第二天。病人已拔除气管插管，半卧位，鼻导管吸氧，已能进少量流质。今天又是小李值班。）

（The tracheal tube was pulled out the second day after the operation. The patient was in a semi-reclining position on the bed, breathing with an oxygen nasal cannula, and could take some fluid. It was Nurse Li on duty again.）

护士：（语气轻快）哟，朱女士，一天没见，这么精神啦。看上去不错。（拉住病人的手）怎么样,胃口好吗？医院的饮食吃得惯吗？

Nurse：（speaking quickly and happily）Hi, Ms. Zhu. I haven't seen you for only one day and you're looking so well（holding the patient's hand）. How is your appetite? I'm afraid you may not be used to the hospital food.

病人：（勉强笑了一下）还可以。

Patient：（smiling reluctantly）The food is fine.

护士：（发现病人的情绪不是很好）是吗？如果吃不惯，可以告诉我们，会改进的。你现在的饮食是营养师特别配制的，经过消毒才能食用，可能口味有点不合，但是对你的恢复是有帮助的。

Nurse：（noticing the patient's mood wasn't very good）Really? You can tell us what you like, and we'll try to improve it. The food is prepared by the dietitians and it has to be sterilized thoroughly. It's good for your recovery but it isn't very tasty.

病人：口味还可以。

Patient：Oh, the taste is OK.

护士：（看见病人眼圈有点红）怎么了，朱女士？见过家人了吗？他们看到你现在这样一定会很高兴！

Part Ⅱ Surgical Nursing Care

Nurse: (noticing the patient's eyes were red) What's the matter? Ms. Zhu, have you seen your family members yet? They will be very happy if they see the progress you've made.

病人:(终于忍不住流下泪)我想他们。能叫他们进来吗?

Patient: (couldn't keep back her tears) I want to see them. Can you call them in?

护士:(为病人擦泪,握紧病人的手,等病人稍稍平静)朱女士,我知道,如果是我,也会希望家人能陪在身边。但是,你现在动了这么大的手术,抵抗力很差。为了减少感染的机会,不能让家人陪伴。等你病情稳定了,转回普通病房,就让他们陪个够,好吗?别哭了,再哭眼睛都红了,就不好看了。(语气转为较轻松)等会儿,我去和主任商量一下,看能不能让你先生在门外看看你,好吗?

Nurse: (wiping tears from the patient's eyes and grasping her hands, after the patient calmed down) Oh, I see. If this happened to me, I would hope my family members could be with me, too. But you know, you have just had an operation and your immune system is very weak. We have to keep your family members away so that you won't be infected. But don't worry. When you are transferred to the regular ward and your situation becomes more stable, you can see them as long as you wish. Try to hold back your tears, OK? If your eyes turn red, you will lose your elegance (speaking jokingly). I will ask the doctor if we can let your husband see you outside the door. Do you want to see him?

病人:好。

Patient: Yes.

护士:但是你要答应我不能太激动喔。

Nurse: But you have to promise me that you won't get too excited.

(经过医师的同意,病人和其先生隔门相见后,情绪稳定,积极配合治疗。)

(The patient saw her husband through the diaphanous door. She

第二部分　外科护患沟通

calmed down some and accepted the treatment willingly.)

情境三/Scene 3

(术后第三天晚上,十点钟,护士小李看见病人在流泪。)

(Nurse Li saw the patient was crying at 10 o'clock on the third day after the operation.)

护士:朱女士,怎么了?还没休息?是哪里不舒服吗(递上纸巾让其擦泪)?

Nurse：Hi, Ms. Zhu, what's wrong? It's time to go to bed. Do you feel uncomfortable(giving her facial tissue to wipe her tears)?

病人:(摇摇头)睡不着,心里不舒服。

Patient：(shaking her head) I can't fall sleep, because I feel miserable.

护士:能跟我谈谈吗?

Nurse：Are you willing to talk about it with me?

病人:我害怕。我在想我的心,这里很难受(指着胸口)。

Patient：I'm scared. I'm thinking of my heart. I feel uncomfortable here (pointing to the center of her chest).

护士:你的心?是原来的那个心吗?

Nurse：Your heart? Do you mean your original heart?

病人:(不说话,只是擦泪)

Patient：(just wiping her tears quietly)

护士:(握住病人的手,郑重地说)朱女士,你知道,你以前的心脏生了病,无法再为你工作了。所以,为了使你能更好的生活,我们把一个健康的心脏移植到你身上。现在这个心脏就是你的,是你新的心脏,是你身体的一部分,你一定要接受它。你的手术这么成功,其实冥冥中就注定这颗心脏是你的。你一定要好起来。你先生、儿子、父母都在等你回去开始新的生活呢!别再胡思乱想了,好吗?

Nurse：(grasping the patient's hand and speaking sincerely) Ms. Zhu, you know that something was wrong with your original heart. It

Part Ⅱ　Surgical Nursing Care

wouldn't work for you any more. So you need a new and healthy heart to replace it. The heart in your chest now indeed belongs to you. It is a part of your body though it is a new member. You need to accept it. The successful operation itself shows that it belongs to you. You will recover very soon. Your husband, your son, and your parents are all wishing to live a new life together with you. So don't think too much. Just relax and get well, OK?

病人：(认真地听着，若有所悟)

Patient：(listening seriously as if she understood)

护士：(又放轻了语气)朱女士，你的反应是正常的。身体上发生这么大的变化是需要一段时间来适应。我希望通过我们一起努力，一切会好起来的。你也是这么想的，是吗？那我们一起加油吧。

Nurse：(speaking softly again) Ms. Zhu, everyone in your situation experiences similar feelings. It will take some time for you to adapt. But everything will be fine. I hope you will cooperate with us. You need to have the same thoughts, OK? Let's continue our efforts together.

病人：(擦干眼泪，用力点点头)好。

Patient：(wiping her tears and nodding her head forcefully) OK.

结果 / Result

病人通过护士不断的鼓励和疏导，开始积极配合治疗，也逐渐接受了移植心脏。10天后病情稳定转普通病房治疗，30天出院。

The patient began to accept the treatment actively under the constant encouragement and counseling of the nurse. She had gradually adapted to the new heart and was transferred to the regular ward after 10 days and left the hospital 30 days later.

第二部分 外科护患沟通

点评 / Comments

心理护理中需要了解所护理对象个体的心理特点,比如年龄、性别、病种以及病人能采取的交流方式。正确分析,对症下药,方能收到良好的效果。这段情景对话中,护士运用热情的鼓励和支持,明确的解答,使病人增加了勇气和期望,激发了其抗病的意志和乐观的精神,获得良好的效果。

During psychological nursing care, we should know the psychological characteristics of the patient for whom we are caring. The characteristics include such items as age, gender, type of sickness and the communication method they can have. We can obtain good outcomes for the patient by careful analysis of these characteristics and apply the proper interventions. In this dialogue, the nurse made the patient regain her courage and hope by using passionate encouragement and supports, and at the same time provided her with clear and precise answers. All of these aroused the patient's hope of overcoming her illness, and the successful outcome.

Part Ⅱ　Surgical Nursing Care

肾移植病人的全程护理
Total Nursing Care for a Patient with Kidney Transplantation

乔美珍　吕金星

背景/ *Background*

小陈在一次出差时,突然晕倒。送到医院检查,发现已是肾功能终末期尿毒症,随后进行了半年的血透。今天配型成功,施行了同种异体肾移植术。

Mr. Chen fainted suddenly while on a business trip. He was sent to a hospital for examination where it was discovered that he was in the last stage of renal dysfunction uremia. After six months' hemodialysis, a matching kidney became available and he underwent an allograft renal transplantation.

情境一/Scene 1

(小陈从手术室返回了病房。)

(Mr. Chen returned to the ward from the operating room.)

第二部分 外科护患沟通

交流 / *Interactions*

护士：小陈，祝贺你手术取得了成功。(小陈试着睁了一下双眼。)

Nurse: Mr. Chen, congratulations on your successful operation. (Mr. Chen tried to open his eyes.)

护士：手术的成功只是移植的第一步。接下来的每一步，都需要得到你的配合，能做到吗？

Nurse: The operation is just the first step to the success of the transplant. We will need your cooperation in the following steps. Could you do that?

病人：能。

Patient: Yes, I can.

护士：现在，请你右下肢保持外展伸直位。(护士扶着陈的右腿。) 对，就这样，请放松。

Nurse: Please extend your right leg and keep it in the straight position. (Nurse helped Mr. Chen in placing his right leg.) Good, keep it like this. Please relax.

病人：需要一直保持这个姿势吗？

Patient: Should I keep it in this position all the time?

护士：不。最好能坚持2天。如果累了，可以移动，但尽可能不要让大腿屈曲，以免影响移植肾的血液供应。

Nurse: No. But you should try to keep it in this position for 2 days. When you feel tired, you may move the leg, but you should try to avoid bending your thigh to prevent disturbing the blood supply to the transplanted kidney.

(术后几小时内，护士小吴帮助小陈翻身，右小腿屈曲。病人生命体征各项指标监护都正常。)

Part Ⅱ Surgical Nursing Care

(During the first few hours after the operation, Nurse Wu helped Mr. Chen to turn his body and bent his right lower limbs. His vital signs and other monitored parameters all appeared normal.)

情景二/Scene 2

(第二天上午,吴来到了陈的病床边。)

(The next morning, Nurse Wu came to Mr. Chen's bedside.)

交流/ Interactions

护士:早上好,非常感谢你的配合,你感觉肛门排气了吗?

Nurse: Good morning. I appreciate your cooperation. Have you passed any gas yet?

病人:是的。肚子里咕噜咕噜地在叫,很饿,想吃东西。

Patient: Yes, I did. I feel hungry, and I want something to eat.

护士:现在可以进食了,但要慢慢地来,先喝口温开水。(陈一口气喝了100 mL。)

Nurse: You may eat now, but take it easy. Have some warm water first. (Mr. Chen drank 100 mL of water.)

病人:进行血透以来,我还没有这样畅快地喝过水。

Patient: I have not drunk water like this since the beginning of the hemodialysis.

护士:如果没有不适,就可进流质饮食了。但请不要马上进牛奶、甜的及含油量高的流质,以免胀气与腹泻。

Nurse: If you don't feel any discomfort, you may start with a liquid diet from now on. Please don't drink milk, sweet drinks or high fat liquid to avoid abdominal distension or diarrhea.

(小吴从流质、半流质以及蛋白质含量着手,指导病人根据肾功能的恢复情况选择合适的饮食,帮助病人度过了手术后的7天。)

第二部分 外科护患沟通

(Based on the recovery of the patient's renal function, Nurse Wu instructed him on food selection, from liquid to semi-liquid diet, and count the amount of protein in the food. She helped the patient go through the first seven days after the operation smoothly.)

情景三/Scene 3

交流/ Interactions

护士：小陈，手术后你恢复得很好。再过几天，你就可以回家了。

Nurse: Mr. Chen, you are recovering very well after the operation. You may go home in a few days.

病人：可以回家了？

Patient: can I go home?

护士：是的，但回家后，希望你能坚持服药，并在饮食、活动及自我监测等方面与我们配合。

Nurse: Yes. But you should keep taking your medication and continue to cooperate with us on your diet, daily activities, and self monitoring.

病人：服药能做到，你只要告诉我该服哪些药就行。

Patient: I will keep taking the medicine. Just let me know which ones I should take.

护士：我知道你行，但服药一定要遵守时间，并定期来院检查，定期监测药物浓度，听从专科医师的嘱咐，调节免疫抑制剂的剂量，万万不能大意随便服药与停药。回家后需要你学会自己检测体温、血压、尿量。当出现体温大于38 ℃、血压增高或尿量突然减少的现象，请及时就诊。

Nurse: I know you can manage. You should also respect the timing for medication, come back to the hospital for the follow-up checks, monitor the drug level on a regular basis, and follow the instructions from the

Part Ⅱ Surgical Nursing Care

specialist to adjust the dosage of the immunosuppressive medication. Please be careful, and don't stop taking medication or take other medications by yourself. You will also need to monitor your body temperature, blood pressure, and urine quantity by yourself. Please see a doctor without any delay when you have a temperature of higher than 38 °C, or a rising of the blood pressure, or an abrupt decrease of the urine.

病人：血压我不会测,怎么办？

Patient: I don't know how to measure blood pressure. What should I do?

护士：没关系,现在开始我来教你。

Nurse: Don't worry. I'm going to teach you now.

结果 / Result

小吴在3天时间内不但教会了小陈及小陈的父亲如何测量血压,同时还让小陈的全家人明白了服用药物、均衡饮食以及适当活动的重要性。半年后的肾友会,小陈找到了他的床位护士小吴,感谢她的帮助,并与小吴谈起了他的体会。

Within three days, Nurse Wu taught Mr. Chen and his father how to measure blood pressure, and she also made it very clear to his whole family about the importance of continuous medication, a balanced diet, and some suitable physical activities. Six months later during a Renal Disease Patients' Group meeting, Mr. Chen looked for Nurse Wu. He expressed his gratitude toward her, and also told her about his experiences.

点评 / Comments

肾移植病人手术前后的护理至关重要。病人的卧位、饮食、服药等将直接影响其预后。本段中护士小吴通过对病人移植前后的全程

第二部分　外科护患沟通

指导和照护以及出院指导,使病人的生存质量得到改善。

　　Nursing care to the patient before and after the kidney transplantation is extremely important. The patient's laying position, his diet, and his medication can directly affect the prognosis. In this episode, Nurse Wu provided a total nursing care to the patient both before and after the transplantation. She also gave the instructions about continues care after discharge. The quality of the patient's life was therefore improved.

Part Ⅱ Surgical Nursing Care

冠脉搭桥术后病人便秘的护理指导
Post-operative Nursing Instructions on Constipation for a Coronary Artery Bypass Graft(CABG) Patient

王莉 曹影婕

背景/ Background

赵女士,教师,患冠心病,行大隐静脉旁路手术。患者平素大便正常,术后因活动减少,食物少纤维,惧怕伤口裂开不敢如厕,术后6天未大便。刘护士适时地来到床边。

Ms. Zhao, a teacher, had CABG surgery because of coronary artery disease. The patient used to have regular bowel movements. Due to a lack of exercise, eating less fibrous meals, and fear of rupturing the incision, she had been afraid to go to bathroom and had not had a bowel movement for six days since the operation. Nurse Liu promptly came to her bedside to talk to her.

交流/ Interactions

护士:赵阿姨,您开刀到现在已经有6天了,您恢复得蛮好的(微

第二部分 外科护患沟通

笑)。对了,您好像很多天没大便了,有什么不舒服吗?

Nurse:Ms. Zhao, it has been six days since you had the operation. You have recovered well (smiling), but it seems that you haven't had a bowel movement for several days. Do you feel uncomfortable?

病人:是的,我是很想上厕所,可我试过,没成功,我怕伤口裂开。

Patient:Yes, I really want to go to the toilet. I've tried but failed, because I'm afraid my incision might become ruptured.

护士:赵阿姨,对于冠心病的手术治疗来说,大隐静脉旁路术是效果最好的一种手术方式。手术以后病人需要做的就是好好休息,增加营养。另外,也要保持大便通畅,防止大便时用力,因为这样会增加心脏负担。您的顾虑我能理解,不过这种伤口一般术后12天就能全部愈合。您已经是第6天了,而且早上我们看过,愈合地挺好的,我想它应该不会影响正常的排便。

Nurse:Ms. Zhao, CABG operation is the most effective method for the coronary artery disease. As a patient who has gone through the operation, you need to have a good rest and increased nutritional intake. At the same time you need to maintain free bowel movements. When you go to the toilet, you should avoid pushing too hard because it can increase the burden on your heart. I can understand your misgivings. Your incision will heal completely in twelve days. Since it has been six days now and this morning we saw that your incision is healing very well, I think it will not be affected by normal defecation.

病人:这样我就放心了,但我已经好几天没上厕所了,估计还是不能很顺利地排出。

Patient:That's good. But I have not been to the toilet for some days. I'm afraid I cannot do it successfully.

护士:别担心,让我来帮您,我先来给您按摩按摩腹部好吗?它可以刺激肠蠕动,促进排便。

Nurse:Don't worry, I can help you. How about letting me massage your abdomen now? It can stimulate the intestines' movement and promote

Part II　Surgical Nursing Care

defecating.

病人：好的，谢谢你。

Patient: All right. Thank you.

护士：(一边按摩一边微笑着说)您这些天不太敢吃蔬菜和水果，是吗？

Nurse: (speaking with a smile while massaging the patient) You haven't eaten any vegetables or fruit recently, have you?

病人：是啊，你怎么知道的？以前我每天都是吃很多水果的，排便一直很正常。但是开完刀后就什么都不敢吃，每天就吃点米饭和鱼汤啊什么的。

Patient: How do you know? I used to eat much fruit and have regular bowel movements. But since the operation I dare not eat anything but rice and fish soup.

护士：难怪您的皮肤这么好！是啊，很多水果和蔬菜都含有大量的维生素和纤维。维生素对身体包括皮肤都有好处，纤维则可以帮助排便，比如香蕉、芹菜、竹笋等。心脏手术跟胃、肠道没什么关系，不用担心。现在吃根香蕉好不好？

Nurse: No wonder your skin is so nice. There are lots of vitamins and fiber in fruit and vegetables. Vitamins are beneficial to your body and skin, and fiber is beneficial to bowel movements. The heart operation has nothing to do with your gastrointestinal tract. So don't worry. How about having a banana now?

病人：好……(开心地笑)谢谢你。

Patient: OK…(smiling) Thanks.

护士：没关系的。(给病人剥好香蕉)为了保持排便通畅，除了多吃纤维含量多的水果、蔬菜，按摩腹部之外，你还可以每天定时去厕所，培养"情绪"。另外，你也要适当下床活动，这对你的康复也是有好处的。

Nurse: It's my pleasure. (peeling a banana) In order to keep free bowel movements, besides eating more fruit and vegetables rich in fiber,

第二部分 外科护患沟通

and massaging your abdomen, you should try to go to the toilet at the same time every day to make it a habit. In addition, you need to get out of bed and move around a little more. It's helpful for your recovery.

病人: 我知道了,听你这么一解释,我放心多了。谢谢你。

Patient: I see. I won't worry any more after your explanation. Thanks a lot.

护士: 不用谢。现在我需要去看别的病人,等会我再来看你,你如果有事就打铃,我会立刻过来的。

Nurse: You are welcome. I need to see another patient now, but I will see you later. You can ring me any time if you need, and I will be right over.

(半小时后护士再次来到床边。)

(Half an hour later, the nurse came to the bedside again.)

护士: 赵阿姨,现在感觉怎么样?

Nurse: How do you feel now, Ms Zhao?

病人: 我刚刚去过卫生间了,你的方法真的很有效。

Patient: I just went to the toilet and had a bowel movement. Your method is very effective.

护士: 你的胃肠道本来就很好,而且你也很愿意配合,所以才会取得这么好的效果。你瞧你到现在体温一直正常,其他情况也都很稳定,像你这样配合,一定很快就会康复的。

Nurse: Your gastrointestinal tract is pretty good and you are willing to cooperate with us. That's why you've achieved such a good result. You see, your temperature has been normal all the time, and other conditions are also stable. I believe you will recover soon.

病人: 太谢谢你了,小刘。

Patient: Thank you very much, Miss Liu.

点评/ Comments

这位护士针对冠脉搭桥术后病人的心理特点,运用了有效的护理

Part Ⅱ Surgical Nursing Care

措施。首先,她肯定了这位病人已积累的自我保健和应对疾病的经验和方式,再对病人的顾虑采取了协商、提醒、暗示等方式与病人进行交流,并辅以护理技能的支持,取得良好的效果。

  Focusing on the psychological characteristics of the patient after CABG, the nurse applied effective nursing interventions. At first, she affirmed the patient's self-health care methods and experiences which the patient has accumulated during her illness. Then she used consulting, reminding, hinting, etc. to communicate with the patient, and she also applied nursing skills to help the patient to achieve good outcome.

第三部分 特殊人群（情境）沟通
Part Ⅲ Nursing Care for Special Patient Groups

第三部分 特殊人群(情境)沟通

一、老年护理
Nursing Care for Senior Patients

老年人跌倒的防护
Preventing the Elderly from Falling Accidents

汪小华

背景/ *Background*

王女士,65岁,退休教师。运动后,下楼时不慎跌倒,顿觉左踝部疼痛难忍,伴恶心。随即坐地上,双手紧捂患处,等待行人经过时扶她起来或送她去医院。此时她的邻居张护士下班回家,路上遇见满脸痛苦状的王老师坐在地上。

Ms. Wang, a 65-year-old retired teacher, fell from the steps while going downstairs after her exercise session. She felt a sharp pain in her left ankle and also felt nauseous. She sat down on the ground, held the injured area and waited for someone to pass by and help her. Miss Zhang, a neighbor of hers who is a nurse was on her way home after work. She found Ms. Wang sitting on the ground with a painful expression on her face.

Part III Nursing Care for Special Patient Groups

交流/ *Interactions*

护士:王老师,您怎么啦?

Nurse: Ms. Wang, what's the matter with you?

病人:哦,是张护士啊。我刚刚下楼时不小心踩了空,当时左脚踝部痛得不得了,还有恶心。

Patient: Ah, Miss Zhang. I fell from the steps when I came downstairs and felt a sharp pain in my left ankle and also felt nauseous.

护士:真是不幸,让我帮您检查一下。(张护士轻轻地扶起她的左腿,先检查左膝关节,无明显异常发现,再检查左踝关节,能活动,但局部疼痛加剧,左下肢各部位无反常活动,无骨擦音。)

Nurse: Oh, I'm sorry to hear that. Let me take a look. (Miss Zhang held Ms. Wang's left leg up gently and checked her knee joint. No abnormality was found. The sore spot was on Ms. Wang's left anklebone and it was more painful when moved. No obvious abnormal movement and crepitate sounds were noticed.)

病人:我是不是骨折了?你快告诉我呀。不过现在疼痛已好了点。

Patient: Please tell me, is there a fracture? The pain is a bit less now.

护士:王老师,您的情况不算严重,从我检查的结果看没有骨折。但是要确定您是单纯的软组织损伤还是伴有骨裂,最好通过摄片后才能确定。

Nurse: Ms. Wang, your injury is not very serious. There does not seem to be a fracture. But you should have an X-ray to ensure whether you just have a soft tissue injury or also a hairline fracture.

病人:如果我有骨裂的话,需要多长时间才能好?

Patient: How long would it take to heal if I have a hairline fracture?

护士:您3周内不能负重。可用石膏托固定受伤踝关节,同时观察局部的血液循环,另外配制一副拐杖,局部进行锻炼,以防关节僵硬

第三部分 特殊人群(情境)沟通

及肌肉萎缩。

Nurse: You shouldn't bear any weight on a hairline fracture for the first 3 weeks. You could need a cast to immobilize your injured ankle. You can use a crutch to help you walk and should monitor the local extremity circulation. Partial exercise helps prevent muscle atrophy and joint stiffness.

病人:好的。

Patient: OK.

护士:您现在怎样了?我现在扶您起来,在边上的凳子上坐一会儿,我们再观察一下好吗?

Nurse: How do you feel now? Let me help you up. Sit down on the bench for a while. We will then monitor the injured ankle a little bit more, OK?

病人:好的。真该死,我的眼睛从年轻时就不好,严重近视,听医生说,现在又有点白内障。

Patient: All right. I have been suffering from severe myopia since I was young, and now my eye doctor told me that I have cataracts.

护士:噢,那您更应该小心。老年人本来视敏度、调节能力和视野下降,加上又有白内障,上下楼梯尤其是下楼梯时更应小心,走路速度要慢。

Nurse: An elderly person like you usually suffers decreased visual acuity, decreased accommodation in the eyes, decreased peripheral vision and is more sensitive to glare. Since you have severe myopia and some cataracts, you should be especially careful when going downstairs and walk slowly.

病人:我有心急的毛病。另外,我锻炼时不要人家在旁边看着我,所以我就选择在人少的地方锻炼。

Patient: I am very impatient. In addition, I select out-of-the-way places for my exercise because I don't like people watching me when I exercise.

Part Ⅲ　Nursing Care for Special Patient Groups

护士：王老师,今后您锻炼时,最好有您的老伴陪着您,这样你们可以互相照应。还有,锻炼时间最好早一点。如果路上光线不好,很容易跌倒的。

Nurse: Ms. Wang, you should ask your husband to accompany you when you exercise so you can take care of each other. Also, the time for you to exercise should be early in the evening before dark. It's easier to fall if there is not enough light.

病人：好的。另外告诉你,我今天多锻炼了一点时间,有点累,这是不是与我跌倒有关?

Patient: Okay. By the may, I also exercised a bit longer today than usual and I was tired. Does this have anything to do with my fall?

护士：可能有关,我认为引起您今天跌倒的原因有好几个呢。

Nurse: Possibly. I think there are several factors that caused your fall.

病人：好的,我会注意的。我现在疼痛好多了,我想回家了。

Patient: I will be more careful in the future. My sore ankle is much better. I want to go home now.

护士：那我扶您回家。

Nurse: Let me accompany you home.

病人：谢谢。

Patient: Thanks.

点评 / Comments

跌倒是老年人尤其是高龄老人(>75 岁)日常生活中经常要发生的事。引起跌倒的原因很多,有病理因素,如感官、心血管、运动及神经系统等疾病;有环境因素,如光线太暗、地面太滑等;有心理因素,如急躁;另外还有自身衣着原因,如裤子太长、鞋不合脚等。老年人跌倒不能马上扶起,应先进行体检,排除骨折和关节严重损伤后才可扶起。王女士的跌倒与她视力不好、急躁、路上光线太暗以及锻炼时间太长有关。

第三部分 特殊人群(情境)沟通

Many elderly persons especially those in senility (> 75 years old) suffer falls in their daily living. The reasons for their falls may be due to: pathological factors, such as special senses disorders, neurological and cardiovascular diseases, muscular-skeletal problems; environmental factor, such as dim and slippery places; psychological factors, such as impatience; and dressing factors, such as trousers that are too long or shoes that are too big. We should not help a fallen elder up before a thorough check. The causes of Ms. Wang's fell were related to poor vision, impatience, a dim pathway, and exercising too long.

Part Ⅲ Nursing Care for Special Patient Groups

老年人的饮食指导
Dietary Instructions for the Elderly

汪小华

 背景/ *Background*

患者殷女士,72 岁,曾有胆囊炎史。因昨晚赴晚宴后 3 小时突感右上腹疼痛,伴呕吐半小时后入院。入院后经身体检查,右上腹有压痛点,墨菲氏征(+),初步诊断为慢性胆囊炎急性发作。第二天清晨,李护士巡视病房时,病人疼痛已明显缓解。

Patient Ms. Yin, 72 years old, has a history of gallbladder disease. She was admitted to the hospital with sudden pain in the right upper abdomen for 3 hours and vomiting for half an hour after participating in a party last night. The physical examination indicated positive Murphy's sign. The diagnosis was an acute episode of chronic cholecystitis. Nurse Li came to see her the next morning and found that the patient's pain had gotten better.

交流/ *Interactions*

护士:殷婆婆,我是您的床位护士,您现在肚子痛好点了吗?

Nurse: Granny Yin, I'm the nurse in charge of your treatment. Is your abdomen pain getting better?

第三部分　特殊人群(情境)沟通

病人:好多了,谢谢你。

Patient: Oh, it's much better now. Thank you.

护士:您昨天晚上是不是在外面馆子吃的晚饭? 您能告诉我您吃了些什么?

Nurse: Did you have supper in a restaurant last night? What kind of food did you have?

病人:我是在外面吃的晚饭,主要吃了点虾、油炸三果、萝卜丝饼,还有蔬菜。

Patient: Yes. I had my dinner last night in a restaurant. I had shrimps, fried nuts, fried radish cake and some vegetables.

护士:您吃得比平时多吗?

Nurse: Did you eat more food last night than usual?

病人:是的,比我平时吃得多,我都感到有点撑了。饭店的菜味道很好。

Patient: Yes, I ate more than usual. I felt so full. The flavor of the restaurant food was wonderful.

护士:虾是水煮的吗?

Nurse: Were the shrimps poached?

病人:不,是椒盐炸虾。

Patient: No, the shrimps were fried.

护士:您平时几点钟吃晚饭?

Nurse: What time do you usually have supper?

病人:大约下午5:30至6点吧。

Patient: About 5:30 to 6:00 pm.

护士:昨天您是不是累了?

Nurse: Were you tired yesterday?

病人:是的,昨天单位里有几个年轻人要问我些问题,我就去了,结果折腾了一天,然后他们就请我一起到餐馆吃晚饭。

Patient: Yes. A few of my younger colleagues invited me to discuss things with them. I was busy with them the whole day. Then they invited

Part Ⅲ Nursing Care for Special Patient Groups

me to have supper with them at the restaurant.

护士:您的胆囊炎以前发作过吗？如有发作,是不是与饮食不当与休息不好有关？

Nurse: Have you suffered from cholecystitis before? If so, were the episodes related to inappropriate diet and rest?

病人:有过两次,都是吃了一碗焖肉面。

Patient: There were two episodes. Both happened after eating a bowl of smoldered meat noodles.

护士:殷婆婆,我有些建议,是针对老年人吃饭方面,尤其是有胆囊和胰腺疾病的。

Nurse: Granny Yin, I have some dietary suggestions for the elders, especially for those who are suffering from chronic cholecystitis or pancreatitis.

病人:是哪些建议呢？

Patient: What suggestions?

护士:老年人每餐应吃得少一点,大约八分饱。饮食宜清淡一点,少吃或不吃油腻和油炸食品。您昨晚吃的油炸三果、萝卜丝饼和椒盐虾都对您的胆囊炎不利。晚饭吃得早一点,不要晚于晚上7点,尤其是您是喜欢早睡的。另外吃饭的速度不能太快,食物切得小一点,做得烂一点,这样有利于您的健康。

Nurse: It's helpful for the elderly not to eat a full meal every time, preferably 80% full. Have light meals, avoid fried or oily food. The fried nuts, radish cake and fried shrimps you had last night are not good for your chronic cholecystitis. Since you like to go to bed early, the time of your supper should be earlier, not later than 7:00 pm. Also, you should not eat too fast, and you should cut the food into smaller pieces, and make them softer. This way is better for your health.

病人:我一天要吃多少蔬菜为好呢？

Patient: How many vegetables should I eat every day?

护士:一天的蔬菜量要达到八两到一斤。因为蔬菜是人体的清道

第三部分 特殊人群(情境)沟通

夫,使您的大便保持通畅。

Nurse: You should have 1/2 pound to 1 pound of vegetables each day. Vegetables are the cleaner for the human body. Adequate dietary fiber is one of the most important factors for bowel function.

病人:我知道了,谢谢。

Patient: I see. Thanks.

点评/ *Comments*

指导老年人饮食要做到以下十点:每餐少一点,八成饱;质量高一点,供应优质蛋白质;蔬菜多一点,每天250g;吃盐少一点,每天6g以下;杂粮多点,不偏食;作料重一点,葱、姜、醋等;饭菜烂一点;粥多喝一点;早餐精一点;晚餐早一点。

Dietary instructions for older people mainly include the following 10 items: Less food per meal, food intake should be 70~80 percent full; protein intake should be high quality; more vegetables, 250 grams per day; take less salt, less than 6 grams a day; more coarse grains with balance diet; more seasoning with onions, ginger or vinegar; cook the meals a little longer, make it softer; more congee; high quality breakfast; earlier time for supper.

Part Ⅲ   Nursing Care for Special Patient Groups

老年性痴呆的护理
Nursing Care for a Patient with Senile Dementia

汪小华

背景/ Background

刘先生,78岁,因进行性遗忘1年伴定向力降低而来就诊。经医生检查,并行脑部CT,初步诊断为老年性痴呆早期。这时门诊护士小张对病人实施健康宣教。

Mr. Liu, 78 years old, went to see a doctor because of progressive memory impairment and disorientation. The doctor's diagnoses combined with a CT scan indicated early stage Alzheimer's disease. Clinical nurse, Miss Zhang, provided health education to the patient.

交流/ Interactions

病人:张护士,我的记忆力越来越坏,近来老是遗忘,有时连我外甥的名字都叫不出来。医生说我得了早期老年性痴呆,听说这个毛病最后会变傻的,实在可怕!

Patient: Miss Zhang, my memory is getting worse. I keep forgetting things. I almost forgot my nephew's name the other day. My doctor told me

第三部分 特殊人群(情境)沟通

that I have early stage Alzheimer's disease. I've heard that people who suffer from Alzheimer's disease will become a fool. It is terrible.

护士：刘大伯，我理解您的想法，但是您先别紧张。您能告诉我您平时一天的生活吗？

Nurse: Mr. Liu, I understand what you are thinking, but don't be nervous. Could you tell me what your daily life is like?

病人：我早晨一般6点钟起床，洗漱后吃早饭，听半小时苏州评弹，看大约一小时电视，和老伴聊聊，就吃中饭。下午打半小时瞌睡(我不敢多睡，怕影响晚上睡觉)，就下楼走一圈，再找个椅子坐会儿，与其他人聊聊天，就回来吃晚饭。晚上与老伴说说话，大约8点钟左右就睡觉了。

Patient: I usually get up at 6 a.m. After brushing my teeth and washing my face, I will have breakfast. Then I enjoy Suzhou Ping Tan for half an hour and watch TV for about one hour. I talk with my wife for some time, and then it will be time for lunch. I usually take a nap for about half an hour (I don't want a long nap because I'm afraid it will affect the quality of night sleep). Then I usually go downstairs for a walk, find a chair to sit down and chat with my neighbors. After that I'll have my supper. I usually go to bed at about 8 p.m.

护士：您平时蔬菜和水果吃得多吗？

Nurse: Do you usually eat enough vegetables and fruit?

病人：吃的，但是不多，我老伴和我一天大约吃八两左右蔬菜吧。我年纪大了，牙齿不好。

Patient: Yes, I do, but not too much. My wife and I eat about half a pound of vegetables every day. I'm old and my teeth are not very good.

护士：您家烧饭用的是什么锅？

Nurse: What kind of cookware do you use?

病人：我家原来用的都是铝锅，后来听说铝锅烧饭对身体不好，我家就将炒菜锅换成铁锅了，但是电饭煲还是铝的。是不是用铝锅不好？

Part Ⅲ Nursing Care for Special Patient Groups

Patient: Originally we used aluminum cookware. Lately, we changed to iron pans because we've heard that aluminum cookware is not good for health. But the electric rice cooker is still made of aluminum. Is it bad to use aluminum cookware?

护士:有研究发现,吃的食物中含铝太多,会导致老年性痴呆。

Nurse: Some researches have found that ingesting excessive aluminum can cause Alzheimer's disease.

病人:真的吗?那我要叫我儿子换个电饭煲了。

Patient: Really? I need to tell my son to change to an electric rice cooker for me.

护士:刘老伯,为了延缓您的病情加重,您平时要多活动。一天只在院子里走一圈是不够的。大公园离您家比较近,您可以打打太极拳,散散步,一天活动的时间增加到2小时左右,但要注意安全。还有要多动脑子,可以帮您的夫人记记日常开支的账,也可打麻将,时间大约1小时左右。还有您的牙齿不好,可将蔬菜和水果切得小一点再吃。

Nurse: Mr. Liu, in order to delay your disease process, you should exercise more. It's not enough just to take a little walk. Since you live near a large park, you can take a walk there or take up shadowboxing to increase your total activities to 2 hours a day. Make sure you pay attention to safety. Try to exercise your brain also. Do some simple calculations such as helping your wife record daily spending, or play mahjong for about one hour. Since your teeth are not very good, you should cut up the vegetables and fruit into smaller pieces before eating them.

病人:谢谢你,那我还有其他需要注意的事吗?

Patient: Thank you. Is there anything else I should pay attention to?

护士:您平时可多吃些鱼,少吃淀粉。帮您夫人干点家务活,这对您的病也是有好处的。

Nurse: You can eat more fish and less starchy food. Helping your wife with household chores is good for you too.

第三部分　特殊人群(情境)沟通

病人：我平时喜欢吃咸鱼,可不可以经常吃?
Patient: I like eating salty fish. Can I eat them often?
护士：您最好少吃咸的食物。您抽烟吗?
Nurse: You should try to avoid salty food. Do you smoke?
病人：有时候要抽的,但没有瘾。
Patient: Yes, sometimes. But I'm not addicted to smoking.
护士：那好,您就戒烟吧!
Nurse: That's good. You should quit smoking all together.
病人：好的,谢谢。
Patient: OK. Thanks.

点评 / *Comments*

预防老年性痴呆和延缓其加重应做到"五多"和"五少",即:多用脑、多干事、多运动、多交往和娱乐、多吃鱼和口香糖;少食铝、少食脂肪、少食盐、少怒、少烟和禁烟。

The measures of prevention and alleviation of Alzheimer's disease consist of "5 more" and "5 less". The "5 more" are: more thinking, more doing, more exercises, more social communication and enjoyment, and eat more fish and chew more gums. The "5 less" are: less aluminum, less fat, less salt intake, less anger, and less smoking and drinking.

Part III Nursing Care for Special Patient Groups

二、小儿患者的护理
Nursing Care for Pediatric Patients

喘息性肺炎患儿的护理
Nursing Care for a Child with Asthmatic Pneumonia

孙丽华　姚文英

背景 / *Background*

患儿王宝宝,男,1岁,因喘息性肺炎发作而住院2天。家长着急,又心疼孩子,加上原有的生活秩序被迫打乱,所以情绪不稳定,孩子一有状况就对医护人员表示不满。

Patient Wang, a one-year old baby boy, was admitted to the hospital two days ago because of asthmatic pneumonia. Worrying about their baby's illness and that their lives routines had been disturbed, the baby's parents had no patience with the doctors or the nurses. As soon as their baby displayed any symptoms, they became upset.

交流 / *Interactions*

护士:您好,王先生,现在要给您的宝宝做氧喷了。
Nurse: Hello, Mr. Wang. It's time to do the nebulization for your baby.

第三部分　特殊人群(情境)沟通

患儿家长：不做！

Patient's Parent：No!

护士：(低头问)怎么啦？

Nurse：(Looking at the baby) What's the matter?

患儿家长：一做氧喷我的孩子就拼命哭，要哭坏了。你看这孩子到医院给你们折腾得，这头上，扎得像马蜂窝似的。

Patient's Parent：My baby will cry loudly as soon as he is given the nebulizer. Since his hospitalization, he has been abused. His head has been punctured with needles so many times. It looks like a beehive.

护士：对不起，我们的感受和您是一样的。心疼孩子生病后受罪，希望孩子早点好。氧喷是治疗喘息性肺炎最好的方法，还可以预防转变为哮喘。要不等他睡着了再做？睡着了做效果也比哭闹时好。

Nurse：Sorry. We have the same feelings as you. We all love the baby and wish him to be cured soon. The nebulization is the best way to treat asthmatic pneumonia and it can also prevent the disease from changing to asthma. How about if we do the nebulization when he's asleep? It's more effective when he is sleeping than when he is crying.

患儿家长：也好，先挂上盐水再说。

Patient's Parent：OK. Go ahead and give him the fluid transfusion first.

(输液开始后。)

(After beginning the transfusion.)

患儿家长：护士，盐水挂上后我的孩子哭得没停过，是不是这个盐水有问题？你们有没有加错药？看病看病，越看病越多，挂了2天水，孩子还是"吼"得很。

Patient's Parent：Nurse, my baby has been crying non-stop since you gave him the transfusion. Are there any problems with the drug you are using? Have you made a mistake? I think he has gotten worse since he came to the hospital. You have given him the fluid transfusion for two days, yet he is still screaming severely.

(护士仔细检查输液及孩子的情况后)

Part Ⅲ Nursing Care for Special Patient Groups

(After examining the baby and the transfusion carefully)

护士:输液没错,孩子哭可能有其他原因。

Nurse: The transfusion is OK. Maybe there are some other reasons for his crying.

患儿家长:肯定今天的盐水有问题,昨天挂并不哭,怎么今天会哭呢?

Patient's Parent: I'm sure there are some problems with the fluid you used today. He did not cry when you gave him the transfusion yesterday. Why is he crying today?

护士:输液中的药我们要两人核对后才能加进去。我去请医生来帮孩子检查一下吧。

Nurse: The drug we used has to be checked twice by two nurses. Let me ask a doctor to examine the baby.

患儿家长:快去,快去,还磨蹭什么?不是你的孩子不知道心疼。什么态度?!

Patient's Parent: Hurry up! What are you waiting for? He is not your baby, so you just do not care about him. What kind of attitude is this?!

护士:对不起,医生会马上来。

Nurse: I'm sorry. The doctor is coming right away.

(医生检查过后,认为还是喘憋引起的烦躁。)

(After examination, the doctor believed the reason for the baby's irritation was wheezing.)

护士:孩子是因为喘了不舒服才哭的。给他用点睡觉的药,尽快将氧喷做了就会好的。氧喷中有缓解气道痉挛的药。

Nurse: The baby feels uncomfortable and is crying because of wheezing. Let's give him a calming drug, and provide the nebulization as soon as possible. He will feel much better after the nebulization. The medication he inhales can relieve the bronchial spasm.

患儿家长:这个药有毒吗?对小孩的副作用大吗?吸了会上瘾吗?是不是每次咳嗽都需要吸药?我们单位效益不好,这费用哪吃得消啊。

Patient's Parent: Is this drug toxic? Does it have any side effects on

第三部分 特殊人群(情境)沟通

children? Is it addictive? Does he need to inhale the drug every time he coughs? My company is not doing well and my salary is not very good. The drug is too expensive for me.

护士:这些药没有毒,无太大副作用,也不会上瘾。回去后做好预防工作,控制住不发也就好了。

Nurse: This drug is not toxic and it isn't addictive. The side effects are small. When your baby is discharged, all you need to do is to avoid another attack.

患儿家长:小孩一生病,我这心里就乱了,恨不得代替他。

Patient's Parent: When my child is sick, I don't know what to do. I wish it was me who is sick, not my baby.

护士:我能理解,孩子睡着了,给他做氧喷吧。

Nurse: I understand. Now your baby is sleeping. Let's give him the nebulization.

点评 / Comments

孩子生病,家属的心情是非常焦急的,希望用药后马上能有效。但是疾病的恢复是一个缓慢的过程,在这期间,怎样缓解家属的焦虑心情,使之配合我们的治疗和护理是非常重要的。所以,我们除了要做好疾病护理,还要实施有效的心理护理,特别是家属的心理护理。

When babies are sick, their parents are always anxious. They wish the diseases can be cured as soon as drugs are used. But the recovery process is usually slow. During this period, it is very important for the nurses to release their worries in order to help them cooperate with the medical staffs. So, the nurses should not only perform disease related nursing care, but also provide psychological nursing care, especially for the baby's parents.

Part Ⅲ Nursing Care for Special Patient Groups

腹泻患儿的护理
Nursing Care for a Child with Diarrhea

周月丽

背景 / Background

女病儿,李佳,8个月,因腹泻住院2天。患儿每天排便10余次,呈黄色水样便,时有哭闹。护士小陆来到床边进行护理。

A female patient, Li Jia, eight-months old, had been in the hospital for two days because of diarrhea. The patient had yellow watery stool more than ten times each day, and cried periodically. Nurse Lu went to care for her.

交流 / Interactions

护士:张姐,宝宝今天大便次数少一点了吗?

Nurse: Good morning, Ms. Zhang. Has the baby's diarrhea been a bit less today?

病儿妈妈:少什么少,还是这么多!你们给我家小孩用的药对不对?

Patient's Mother: No, still a lot. Are the drugs you used for my child correct?

第三部分　特殊人群(情境)沟通

护士：我们对每一位病人都是负责的。每种疾病的治疗都有一定的原则。药物的剂量是根据宝宝的年龄和体重计算的,请您放心!

Nurse: We are responsible for every patient. There are certain principles to the treatment of every disease. The dosage of the drug is calculated according to the baby's age and weight. Please don't worry.

病儿妈妈：呵,我怎么能放得下心!我最不放心的就是怕你们给耽误了!

Patient's Mother: How could I not worry! What I'm concerned about most is that you might have delayed her treatment.

护士：我能理解您的心情,请相信我对您说的都是心里话。俗话说,"病去如抽丝",疾病好转都有一个过程。您宝宝得的是病毒性肠炎。一般来说,病毒感染的疾病要一周左右的时间,才会好转。

Nurse: I can understand how you feel. Please believe me that what I said to you is from my heart. People used to say "To recover from an illness is like reeling off raw silk from the cocoons." It will take a certain process for patients to become better. What your baby has is viral enteritis, and in general, a virus infected disease needs about one week or more to recover.

病儿妈妈：呦,你看,小孩又拉了,快去喊医生过来。(孩子哭。)

Patient's Mother: Look, the child has diarrhea again. Call the doctor quickly. (The baby is crying.)

护士：好,您别着急!我马上去喊医生。

Nurse: OK, don't worry. I will call the doctor right away.

(医生检查后,认为粪便中的水分减少了,病情有好转。)

(After examing the baby, the doctor thought the water content in the stool had decreased, the illness had taken a favorable turn.)

病儿妈妈：又说好!我就知道你们不心疼孩子。

Patient's Mother: You keep saying the illness is getting better. I know you do not care about my child.

护士：这里的医生都是很有经验的。刚才医生还用试剂测试了一

Part Ⅲ Nursing Care for Special Patient Groups

下粪便的酸碱度,情况确实是好多了。

Nurse: The doctors here are all very experienced. The doctor who examined your child also tested the acid-based concentration of her excrement. The situation is really much better.

(家属准备给孩子换尿布。)

(The baby's mother prepared to change the diaper for the child.)

护士:张姐,我来帮您。

Nurse: Ms. Zhang, let me help you.

(护士用温水给孩子清洗臀部,换上干净的尿布。)

(The nurse washed the buttock of the baby with warm water and put on a clean diaper.)

护士:张姐,宝宝的大便情况好多了。不过,还是要继续喂去乳糖奶粉。这样容易消化,有利于肠黏膜的修复。您最近阶段的饮食要清淡,这样奶水中的脂肪含量也能少一些。另外,你要给宝宝多喂水,补充宝宝所需的水分。

Nurse: Ms. Zhang, the baby's stool is much better. But she still should be fed with lactose free milk powder. It is easy to digest and is good for the intestinal mucous membrane to repair. Also, your diet should be light at the present time, so that there will be less fat in your breast milk. In addition, you should give more water to the baby to supplement the baby's water need.

病儿妈妈:你的态度还算是不错。

Patient's Mother: Your attitude is not too bad.

护士:谢谢,宝宝好像是要睡觉了,待会我再来看宝宝。

Nurse: Thank you. The baby is about to sleep. I will come to see her later.

(2个小时后,护士第二次来到床边。)

(Two hours later, the nurse came back a second time to her bedside.)

病儿妈妈:小陆啊,宝宝已经2个小时没拉了。我现在放心多了,谢谢。

第三部分　特殊人群(情境)沟通

Patient's Mother: Thank you very much, Nurse Lu. My baby has not had a bowel movement for two hours. I feel much better now.

点评/ Comments

　　这位宝宝的妈妈的不和善态度是因为对疾病知识的缺乏,导致焦虑和恐惧的心理。这位床位护士能够换位思考,用耐心帮助的方法去缓解矛盾。优秀的儿科护士与病人家属必须建立有效的沟通。

　　The reason for Ms. Li's unpleasant attitude was due to her lacking knowledge about the disease which caused her to be anxious and frightened. This nurse resolved the conflict by thinking from Ms. Li's point of view to explain things and to help them. A good pediatric nurse should be able to establish good communication with the patient's family members.

Part Ⅲ Nursing Care for Special Patient Groups

肺炎患儿的护理
Nursing Care for a Child with Pneumonia

阐玉英　汤文决

背景 / Background

患儿,女,7个月,因"咳嗽十天,发热一天"而收入院。患儿阵发性咳嗽,有痰,中等度发热,且病程比较长,家长特别紧张。护士小吕来到床边进行护理。

A 7-month old baby girl was hospitalized after coughing for ten days and had a fever for one day. The baby had a paroxysmal cough, sputum, and a moderate fever. The baby's parents felt nervous because they thought their daughter's symptoms had lasted too long. Nurse Lv came to the baby's bedside to care for her.

交流 / Interactions

护士:大姐,今天宝宝咳嗽好一点了吗?

Nurse: Mrs. Li, is your baby getting any better?

患儿家长:没好,反而咳得更厉害了! 挂了三四天的水,一点效果都没有。

Patient's Parent: No, she seems to be getting worse. She has had the intravenous transfusion for 3 – 4 days without any improvement.

第三部分　特殊人群(情境)沟通

护士:咳嗽是不是感到松一点了?
Nurse: Is her coughing better?

患儿家长:是的。
Patient's Parent: Yes.

护士:有的孩子肺炎初期只是阵发性干咳,但随着时间的推移,崩解的粒细胞和被杀死的细菌、病毒形成痰液,刺激支气管引起阵发性咳嗽、咳痰。就像战场上打仗,会有许多敌人的尸体。其实痰液就是清理战场的产物,是疾病发展的自然过程。您不要太着急,我们正在积极治疗。药物发挥作用也要一段时间,再观察观察好吗?

Nurse: Some babies have a dry paroxysmal cough at the early stage of pneumonia. As time goes on, the disintegrated and dead bacteria and virus become sputum, which will stimulate the broaches and result in a paroxysmal cough and sputum. It's like a battlefield where lie many dead enemy soldiers. Sputum is the waste product that is being cleaned from the body's respiratory system. There is a disease development process. You should not worry too much. We are giving the baby a very effective treatment, but it takes time for the drugs to take effect. Let's try to be a little more patient, OK?

患儿家长:都十多天了,现在就一个孩子,我们心里急啊。
Patient's Parent: We are very worried for our only baby since she has been ill for more than 10 days.

护士:我理解您的心情,但着急解决不了问题,反而影响您自身的抵抗力。到时候不要孩子好了,您倒下了,反过来再传染给孩子,那就更不合算了。您也要注意多休息,多摄取营养丰富的食物,以增强抵抗力。

Nurse: I can understand how you feel. However, your worries cannot solve any problems. It will even affect your own immune system. You should take better care of yourself otherwise you'll get sick, which in turn will affect your baby's health. So you should get some rest and eat some nutritious food to increase your resistance to the diseases.

患儿家长:那我平时要注意些什么?
Patient's Parent: Then what should I pay attention to?

Part III Nursing Care for Special Patient Groups

护士：平时您要注意保持室内空气新鲜,经常开窗通风。宝宝咳嗽的时候,及时拍背帮助他把痰液咳出来。拍背时注意五指并拢内屈,使手掌边缘同时接触孩子的背,引起振动,借重力作用帮助痰液排出(同时示范拍背的方法)。像您的孩子不会吐痰出来一般都咽到肚子里去了,有时你会看到大便中有黏胨样的东西,那就是痰液。

Nurse: At home you should open the windows often to keep the air fresh. When your baby coughs, pat her back softly to help her cough up the sputum. When patting, you should close your five fingers of your hand and pat on the baby's back with only the edge of the hand. Pat her softly and let the vibration from the patting help the baby cough up her sputum (demonstrating how to pat). Since your baby is too young to spit, she can only swallow it. When you find some mucus in her stool, it's the sputum she had swallowed.

患儿家长：是啊,我还以为吃坏了呢。

Patient's Parent: Oh, now I see. I thought it was the bad food she ate.

护士：是的,有的孩子由于痰液刺激胃肠道或者是病毒本身的作用,有时还要拉肚子呢！不过您不要太紧张,并不是每一个孩子都会拉肚子的。现在您的宝宝还有点发烧,我们会4小时给她量一次体温。您若觉得宝宝身体烫,随时叫我们来量体温,假如体温过高,医生会让宝宝吃退烧药的,但您不要自己觉得她发烧了就随便给她吃。平时多给宝宝喝点水,出汗多时要及时更换衣服,或在背上垫一块干的毛巾,防止着凉。我过一会儿再来看宝宝,您有事请按铃。

Nurse: Sometimes the sputum stimulates the gastrointestinal track or due to viral effects, some babies will have diarrhea. But you need not worry too much because not every baby has diarrhea. Since your baby has a fever, we'll take her temperature every 4 hours. Please call us to measure her temperature at any time if you feel she has a fever. If her temperature is too high, the doctor will give her an antipyretic drug. Please don't give her any medication yourself. Feed your baby more water and change her clothes when she is perspiring too much. You may put a dry towel on her

第三部分　特殊人群(情境)沟通

back to prevent her from catching cold. I will come around some time later. You may press the call button to call us if you need.

(第 2 天)

(Next day)

护士：您的宝宝好多了。以后要注意冷暖，及时根据季节变化增减衣服，少去公共场所，注意喂养，及时添加辅食。

Nurse：Your baby is much better now. After you get back home, you should check her clothing, add or reduce her clothes with the changing seasons. Avoid going to public places with your baby when possible. Pay attention to your baby's nutrition and add supplemental food when needed.

患儿家长：谢谢你，我孩子现在咳嗽少多了，我们也放心了。

Patient's Parent：Thank you very much. The baby is coughing much less now. We are not worried any more.

点评/ Comments

7 个月的婴儿，虽然对生病住院的心理反应较小，可是家属的心理反应却甚大。案例中的护理人员非常同情和理解他们的紧张、急躁情绪，并采用加强沟通、交流的正确方法。这样的护理措施起到了良好的安抚教育作用，也取得了家属的信任和配合。

A 7-month-old baby has less psychological responses when hospitalized, but the child's parents usually have much severe psychological responses. In this episode the nurse understood and sympathized with the parent's anxiety. She also correctly applied the methods for strengthening interaction and communication. These nursing interventions played a good role in educating and calming down the parent, and also won the parent's trust and cooperation.

Part Ⅲ   Nursing Care for Special Patient Groups

三、感染病患者的护理
Nursing Care for Patients with Infectious Diseases

人工肝治疗病人的术前宣教
Pre-procedure Instructions for a Patient with Artificial Liver Treatment

吴玉芳

背景 / Background

病人王先生,29 岁,大学文化。因慢性重症肝炎入院。明日上午将接受人工肝支持治疗。因为对此项新疗法缺乏进一步了解,所以心理非常紧张,于是他找到责任护士。

A 29-year old patient, Mr. Wang is a college graduate. He was admitted to the hospital because of chronic severe hepatitis. He was scheduled to receive supporting artificial liver treatment the next morning. Not knowing much about this procedure, he was very nervous. So he went to talk to his nurse.

交流 / Interactions

病人: 我很担心明天的人工肝手术,这个手术到底是怎样的? 我是不是一定要做人工肝?

Patient: I'm very concerned about the upcoming artificial liver opera-

第三部分 特殊人群(情境)沟通

tion. Can you tell me about it? Must I receive this operation?

护士：我理解你这种担心。因为这是一种新的治疗技术，让我给你做一个详细介绍吧。

Nurse: I understand your concern. It is a new therapeutic technique. Let me give you detailed information.

病人：那太好了。

Patient: That's great.

护士：人工肝是用特殊仪器把人体的血液引出，经过分离、吸附，把血液中的黄疸素和毒素等有害物质去除，使肝细胞能再生及恢复，帮助病人渡过肝炎危险期。因为此项技术代替了肝脏的部分功能，所以称人工肝。这不是一项手术，是一种内科治疗方法，需要在专门的人工肝治疗室进行。

Nurse: An artificial liver uses special equipment to draw blood out of the body and removes harmful substances such as bilirubin and toxin from the blood by means of separation and absorption. It will help the liver cells to regenerate and recover, and thus helps the patient pull through the critical stage. Since this technique replaces some of the liver functions, we call it an artificial liver. It isn't an operation but a medical treatment, which must be proceeded in a special artificial liver room.

病人：原来是这样，那我的病是不是已经很重，一定要做人工肝呢？

Patient: I see. Is my disease so serious that I have to have this treatment?

护士：根据你的症状和化验结果，我们诊断为重症肝炎。这一型肝炎病情发展迅速，肝细胞会大量坏死。预后一般较差，但如果采取有效措施，应用暂时支持手段维持，等待肝细胞的再生，帮助你度过危险期，康复的希望是很大的。人工肝正是这种有效的支持手段。

Nurse: According to your symptoms and the laboratory test results, you are suffering from severe hepatitis. This situation develops rapidly: many liver cells die, and the prognosis is generally bad. But if we take

Part III Nursing Care for Special Patient Groups

some effective measures and apply temporary supporting steps to sustain your life and wait for the regeneration of liver cells, it will help you pull through the critical stage. There is great hope for your recovery. An artificial liver is the most effective supporting measure.

病人: 真的? 那做人工肝疼吗? 有危险吗?

Patient: Really? Is this treatment painful, and is it dangerous?

护士: 通常情况下,在人工肝的治疗过程中,我们会用仪器监测你的脉搏、呼吸、血压、心电图,会给你吸氧。治疗过程中,你可能会出现四肢麻木、抽搐、皮疹、皮肤瘙痒、发冷、头晕、恶心、呕吐、腹痛等。这些症状我们都会重视并进行处理的,一般都能缓解。至于疼痛,因为要把你的血引出来,我们会根据你的血管情况在你颈部或腹股沟静脉内插根管子,插管前会用局部麻药,所以通常是不会很疼的。

Nurse: During the treatment, we will monitor your pulse, respiration, blood pressure and ECG and give you oxygen. There are some side effects such as limb numbness, convulsion, skin rash, feeling cold, light-headedness, nausea or vomiting, and abdominal pain. We will take measures to deal with these symptoms and generally they will be relieved. It depends on the condition of your veins. We will insert a cannula tube into your jugular vein or femoral vein to draw blood from your body. It is usually not painful because we will use a local anesthetic before inserting the cannula tube.

病人: 那我就放心了。我自己需要注意哪些问题来配合治疗呢?

Patient: This sets my mind at ease. What do I need to do to cooperate with you for this treatment?

护士: 真高兴你对治疗持有这样的积极态度。在人工肝治疗前,你最好先训练一下在床上大小便。一般认为,治疗次数最好在三次以上才能取得良好的效果。所以第一次治疗结束后,静脉插管要留着,特别是股静脉插管,起床大小便容易牵拉管子,造成出血、脱管等意外,因此人工肝治疗后要卧床休息。其次,明天上午去人工肝室前要排空大小便,以免治疗过程中有便意。再有,今晚睡眠一定要充足,这

第三部分 特殊人群(情境)沟通

样才能保证治疗前的精力充沛啊。

Nurse: It is great that you have such a positive attitude towards this treatment. First, prior to treatment, you should train yourself to urinate and have bowel movements while lying in bed. Generally, you need to receive these treatments at least 3 times for the best results. After the first treatment, the tube remains inserted in your vein. If you get up to urinate or have a bowel movement, the tube may be stretched and lead to bleeding, especially for the femoral vein. So patients need to stay in bed after the artificial liver treatment. Second, you must empty your bladder and stool before going to the ALSS room tomorrow morning, avoiding the need for elimination during the treatment. Third, you should have enough sleep tonight so you will have enough strength for the treatment tomorrow.

病人:好的,我记住了。

Patient: OK, I'll do that.

护士:另外,你今晚最好洗个澡,因为静脉导管留置期间不能洗澡,以免潮湿污染伤口。不过你洗澡时注意不要受凉,不要太疲劳好吗?

Nurse: Also, you should take a bath this evening, because you can't take a bath with the cannula in place. This is to prevent contamination of the insertion site. Be careful not to catch a cold when taking a bath and do not become too tired.

病人:好的,听了你的一番介绍,我心里的石头总算落地了,谢谢你。

Patient: Yes, your explanation relieves my worries. Thank you.

点评/ Comments

由于护士确认了病人的紧张和焦虑的来源,并给予了有效的解释,使病人消除了疑虑,以良好的心态迎接第二天的治疗。解释是心理护理的基本技术之一,旨在帮助病人澄清疑虑,增强信心。有效的解释是指病人能够接受的说服,是在了解病情和病人心理特征的基础

Part Ⅲ Nursing Care for Special Patient Groups

上"摆事实,讲道理",针对病人焦虑的问题,运用通俗易懂的言语,以商量的态度、充足的理由进行说服。

The nurse understood the patient's stress and anxiety, provided effective explanations which helped the patient to relieve his misgivings, and allowed him to wait for the next day's treatment with a better mood. Explanation is one of the basic techniques of psychological nursing, which aims at helping the patients to relieve their misgivings and increase their confidence. Effective explanation is a persuasion that patient can accept. It should be based on understanding the patients' illness and their characteristics, and focus on the patient's anxiety, use the straightaway language, and have an attitude of discussion and persuasion with sufficient reasoning.

第三部分 特殊人群(情境)沟通

重症肝炎病人的意识评估
Evaluating the Level of Consciousness for a Patient with Severe Hepatitis

吴玉芳

背景/ *Background*

病人张先生,40岁,因亚急性重型肝炎入院。病人高中文化,性格内向,平日话语不多。近日病人自觉乏力加重,睡眠差,皮肤巩膜明显黄染。今日血生化报告提示总胆红素408 mmol/L,谷丙转氨酶轻度升高。床位护士下午巡视病房时,与病人进行交谈。

Patient Mr. Zhang, 40 years old with a senior school education. He was admitted to the hospital for sub-acute severe hepatitis. The patient has an introverted personality and is usually very quiet. Recently his fatigue was more serious. His biochemical examination results today showed that his total bilirubin count was 408 mmol/L, and his GTP was also slightly increased. His nurse had the following conversations with him when she made her rounds of the unit that afternoon.

交流/ *Interactions*

护士:老张,你今天感觉怎么样?胃口好吗?

Part Ⅲ　Nursing Care for Special Patient Groups

Nurse: Mr. Zhang, how do you feel today? How is your appetite?

病人:今天感觉不错,胃口比前两天好多了。中午家里给我炖了一只小甲鱼,我一口气就把它吃光了。晚上我太太准备再给我做些好吃的来。

Patient: Well, my appetite today is better than the last couple of days. My wife stewed a turtle for me for lunch and I ate the whole thing. She is going to prepare some tasty food for me this evening as well.

护士:是吗!你太太真贤惠。

Nurse: Is that right! Your wife is so nice.

病人:是的,我这次生病可苦了她了,除了上班还要跑医院。小吴护士,我这病还需住院多长时间?这样我太太要累垮的。

Patient: Yes, my disease has made her suffer very much. She has to work and take care of me. How long do I have to stay in the hospital? If it's too long, my wife may become sick due to the hard work.

护士:老张,你别心急。你住院还不到一个星期,医生正在用最好的方案给你治疗。不过有一点我要跟你重申一下,目前你的疾病处于发展阶段,饮食要清淡,不宜太油腻,增加营养固然是好的,但目前不要进食太多高蛋白食物,像甲鱼、鳗鱼、鸡蛋等暂时不要吃,等你的病慢慢恢复了,肝功能指标正常了,再适当补充蛋白质好吗?

Nurse: Relax, Mr. Zhang, so far you have only been here for one week. Your doctor is treating you with the best program. One important thing I need to remind you of is that your disease is still in the progressive stage. Your food should be very light, and too much fat is not good for you. Supplemental nutrition is good, but at the present time you should avoid food containing high protein such as turtles, eels, eggs, etc. After you have recovered and the index of your liver function is normal, you may then supplement with protein.

病人:噢!我忘了你跟我说过的,那我暂时先不吃。

Patient: Oh, I forgot what you said before. I won't eat those foods from now on.

第三部分 特殊人群(情境)沟通

护士:这一点非常重要,老张,你务必要牢记了。这两天你没有解大便,可以吃一些粗纤维的食物和水果,譬如芹菜、茭白等。适当多喝点水。还有,每天可在脐周顺时针方向按摩 3 次,每次 5~10 分钟,这样可以促进排便。我会请医生开一些促进排便的药物给你。

Nurse: This is very important. You must keep it in mind. You haven't had bowel movements for two days, so you should eat some fruit and vegetables that are rich in fiber such as celery, and cane shoot etc. You should also drink proper amount of water. In addition, you may massage your abdomen area around the belly button in a clockwise direction three times a day, 5 – 10 minutes each time. This can promote bowel movements. I will also ask your doctor to prescribe some medication for your bowel movements.

病人:谢谢你,小吴护士,今天晚上我让太太烧些蔬菜来。

Patient: Thank you, Miss Wu. I will ask my wife to cook some vegetable dishes tonight.

(晚上,护士交接班巡视病房时,病人老张很热情地跟接班护士打招呼。)

(In the evening, when the nurse made her unit rounds during shift exchange, Mr. Zhang greeted the nurse enthusiastically.)

病人:小林护士,你今天值晚班,真是挺辛苦,我向你致敬。护士崇高而伟大,在万家灯火的夜晚,你们守护在病人身边,鼓励我们,给我们指导。等我出院后,我要写诗来歌颂你们。

Patient: Ms. Lin, you are working the night shift. It's a hard job and I salute you. Nurses are so great. They take care of us, encourage us and instruct us even at night time when everyone else is resting at home. I will write poems to praise you after I leave the hospital.

(交接班时,护士小吴曾向小林交代了病人老张的情况,包括生化报告、饮食、排便情况。小林觉得老张今天很健谈,跟以往有所不同,回答说)

(During a shift change, Nurse Wu had told Nurse Lin about Mr.

Part Ⅲ Nursing Care for Special Patient Groups

Zhang's conditions, including his biochemical test results, diet, eliminations of urine and stool. She noted that Mr. Zhang is very talkative today and is not the same as before. Nurse Lin said to him)

护士:老张,谢谢你,你能理解我们的护理工作,真让我高兴。现在你能配合我做一些检查吗?

Nurse: Thanks, Mr. Zhang. Your understanding of our work makes me very happy. Now will you cooperate with me to do some tests on you?

病人:非常愿意。

Patient: Certainly.

护士:你两臂平伸,肘关节固定不动,手掌向背侧伸展,手指分开。(小林边说边演示,老张按护士的指导伸出手臂,护士发现病人的手向外侧偏斜,掌指关节、腕关节有不规则的扑击样抖动,她说)

Nurse: Stretch out your arms and keep them level. Don't move your elbow joints, stretch your palms backward and open your fingers like this. (Nurse Lin demonstrated as she talked. Mr. Zhang stretched his arms under the nurse's guidance. The nurse noticed that his hands leaned outwards and his palm-finger joints and his wrist joints had flipping tremor. She said)

护士:好的,你做得不错,接下来,我们来做几道算术题好吗?

Nurse: Good, you did well. Now let us do some math problems, OK?

病人:你把我当成小朋友啦(笑着说),那好吧。

Patient: You are treating me like a child (saying with a smile). All right.

护士:3 + 7 等于多少?

Nurse: What is 3 plus 7?

病人:等于10。

Patient: 10.

护士:13 + 18 等于多少?

Nurse: What is 13 plus 18?

病人:(老张想了一会儿)等于20。

第三部分 特殊人群(情境)沟通

Patient:(He thought for a few seconds)20.

护士:6+7等于多少?

Nurse:What is 6 plus 7?

病人:等于10。

Patient:10.

护士:好的,老张,你答得不错,现在你先休息。等一下我会来给你抽一个血,做一些化验。

Nurse:OK, Mr. Zhang, your answers are fine. Take a rest now. I will draw some blood from you later so we can run some tests for you.

病人:谢谢你小林。

Patient:Thank you, Ms. Lin.

结果 / Result

护士观察到病人有性格改变、计算能力下降,并出现扑翼样震颤,结合病人有便秘、高蛋白饮食、测血氨高于正常范围,初步确认病人处于肝昏迷前驱期,立即汇报医生。经降血氨、灌肠、禁食蛋白质等及时治疗后,病人神经系统症状好转,血氨恢复正常,避免了肝昏迷的发生。

The nurse detected the changes of the patient's character, declining computing power, and he had flipping tremor. Combining the patient's constipation, high protein diet, and his elevated blood ammonia level, she affirmed that the patient was in the prodromal stage of liver coma and reported it to the doctor at once. With prompt treatments such as decreasing the level of blood ammonia, enema, stopping high protein diet, the patient's neural symptom took a turn for the better and the occurrence of liver coma was avoided.

点评 / Comments

观察是一种有目的、有计划、比较持久的知觉。敏锐的观察能力是护士必须具备的品质之一,是源于注意、记忆、分析、判断等心理活

Part Ⅲ Nursing Care for Special Patient Groups

动的综合应用。护理人员在工作过程中,必须养成运用视、听、触、嗅等感官,随时有目的地、系统地感知护理对象的动作、表情、言语等外显行为所提示的内在变化,正确认识和判断他们的需求,使护理措施有预期的主动性。

Observation is a purposive, planned and persistent perception. Keen observation is one of the necessary characters that nurses must have. It is stemmed from integrated application of mental activities such as attention, memory, analysis and judgment. Nurses must use all their sensory organs at all times to form a habit of planned and systemic perception to their patients' internal changes that can be tracked from the patients' external behaviors like actions, emotions, speeches, etc. They must correctly understand and evaluate the patients' needs, and make nursing care with proactive interventions.

第三部分　特殊人群(情境)沟通

肝炎病人的休息指导
Instructions on Resting for a Hepatitis Patient

吴玉芳

背景/ *Background*

病人刘先生,26岁,中专文化。因急性肝炎入院,治疗一月余准备明日出院。小刘对出院后如何正确掌握活动量心中无数,于是他向他的护士询问此问题。

Patient Mr. Liu, 26 years old with a technical secondary school education. He was admitted to the hospital for acute hepatitis. After one month of treatment, he was going to be discharged from the hospital the next day. However, he had no ideas about the proper amount of activity for himself, so he asked his nurse about this issue.

交流/ *Interactions*

病人:我明天要出院了。我知道得了肝炎要多休息,不知道要休息多长时间才能正常上班?

Patient: I'll be discharged from the hospital tomorrow. I know that patients suffering from hepatitis need a lot of rest. But I don't know how

Part Ⅲ Nursing Care for Special Patient Groups

long I should rest before I can work normally.

护士:小刘,恭喜你可以出院了。出院以后你的确要注意休息,包括精神休息和身体休息。要增加休息时间,减轻体力消耗,减轻肝脏负担。

Nurse: Congratulations. You certainly need to pay attention to rest after leaving the hospital. You should pay attention to both physical and mental rest. You should increase the time for rest and decrease the consumption of physical strength to relieve the burden of your liver.

病人:什么是精神休息呢?

Patient: What is a mental rest?

护士:精神休息就是说你的精神要放松,心情要平和。工作、学习、家务、人际方面的事情要暂时放开。

Nurse: Mental rest means that mentally you should relax, and maintain a peaceful mindset. Set aside your office work, study, housework, and social activities temporarily.

病人:不工作、不学习、不交际,岂不是很闷?

Patient: Without work, study, and social activities, life would become very boring.

护士:不会啊,你可以根据自己的爱好听听音乐、写写日记、养养花草,但是精神过分集中的事情不要做,比如上网聊天、打牌、玩游戏机等。

Nurse: Life wouldn't be very boring. You could listen to music, keep a diary or do lightweight gardening. But you must not do things that will preoccupy yourself excessively, such as chatting on line, playing card games, playing game machines, etc.

护士:遵命。那么身体方面的休息要注意些什么呢?

Patient: OK. How should I follow the physical rest instructions?

护士:你患的是急性肝炎。据统计,95% 的急性肝炎能治愈,但是过度劳累、睡眠不足都会影响恢复。所以你出院后至少一个月内要在家休息,不能上班,生活要有规律。一个月后可以做一些力所能及的

第三部分 特殊人群(情境)沟通

事情,如洗碗、擦灰、整理房间等。如果你上班的工作量不是很大,你可以试着去工作,从半天开始,根据身体状况逐渐恢复至全天工作。如果上班工作量较大,你最好去跟领导商量,暂时更换一个较轻松的岗位。在出院后的半年内,一定要避免过度劳累。

Nurse: You are suffering from acute hepatitis. Ninety five percent of patients with this disease can be cured according to the statistics. However, excessive fatigue and inadequate sleep will influence the recovery. So for at least the first months after you leave the hospital, you must rest at home. You must not go to work. Your life must be regular. After one month you can do some moderate work such as washing dishes, dusting, and tiding the room. If your job workload is not very heavy, you may try to work. At the beginning you could work for half a day and gradually restore full time duties according to your recovery condition. If your workload is heavy, then you should consult with your supervisor to temporarily shift you to an easier job. You must avoid excessive fatigue in the first six months after you leave the hospital.

病人:好的,我去跟领导说说,他很有人情味的。

Patient: OK. I will consult with my boss. He is quite considerate.

护士:还有一点很重要,就是在你恢复期内,要尽量安排午睡,这是解除疲劳、恢复体力的极佳方法。午睡时间以 0.5~1.5 小时为好。另外,睡觉以右侧卧位为宜,使身体与床面成 45 度角。

Nurse: Another important thing is that you must have a midday nap which should last about 30 minutes to one and a half hours. This is the best method to relieve fatigue and restore physical strength. Furthermore, it is better to lie on your right side, and maintain a 45-degree angle while you sleep.

病人:为什么呢?

Patient: Why?

护士:因为这种卧位使肝脏位于腹腔动脉的下方。动脉血液走下行路线流向肝脏,这对动脉血为肝脏输送营养物质十分有利。

Part Ⅲ   Nursing Care for Special Patient Groups

Nurse: Because this lying position puts the liver under the celiac artery and allows the blood to flow down to the liver. It is more beneficial for the transporting of nutritious substances from the artery to the liver.

护士:原来,休息还有那么多讲究,我一定会按你的指导去做的。

Patient: Oh. There are so many details regarding rest. I will follow your guidance.

护士:是的,休息对肝炎病人尤其重要。人们说肝病三分治疗、七分休养,可见休息的重大意义。任何时候,如果你感觉疲劳,一定不要硬撑,要学会休息,同时要定期去门诊复查肝功能,监测肝脏恢复情况。

Nurse: Yes, relaxation is especially important to patients with hepatitis. Many people say that the treatment of hepatitis includes 30% therapy and 70% rest. This shows the importance of rest. If you feel tired at any time, please don't insist on working. You must learn how to rest and be sure to go to the hospital outpatient department to reexamine the liver function periodically so that you can monitor the recovery of your liver.

病人:谢谢你,今天为我上了一堂生动的休息课,让我受益匪浅。

Patient: Thank you for your lively lecture about rest. It will benefit me much.

点评 / Comments

这位护士的休息指导是理想的。在整个指导过程中洋溢着护患双方共同参与的良好氛围。护理人员用分享康复快乐的开场白调动了护理对象的积极情绪,激发了他进一步配合治疗的愿望。在交谈过程中,双方既是提问者,又是回答者,护理对象不是被动地接受护理,而是积极主动地配合和参与护理活动。在这里,护理人员正确接受反馈信息的同时,不断提供高工作质量,表现出一种新型的平等合作关系。

The instruction about rest given by this nurse is ideal. There is a good climate for the nurse and the patient to work together in the whole instruc-

第三部分 特殊人群(情境)沟通

tional process. The prologue the nurse used—sharing happiness of recovering with the patient, evoked active emotion of the nursing client and helped him raise his desire to cooperate with the medical personnel during treatment. In the entire conversation process, the two parties are both questioner and responder. The patient did not receive instructions passively but took part actively. The nurse properly received feedback and continued to provide high quality of work. This shows the new, equal, and collaborative nurse-patient relationship.

Part III   Nursing Care for Special Patient Groups

四、精神或心理问题的护理
Nursing Care for Patients with Psychiatric or Mental Problems

焦虑症病人的护理
Nursing Care for a Patient with Anxiety Neurosis

赵惠英

背景 / Background

吴女士,41岁,因睡眠差、紧张、焦虑、坐立不安而入院。经药物治疗后,焦虑症状改善。医生考虑减少催眠药物的剂量,可是病人出现了明显的焦虑不安,担心晚上减了药后会睡不着。于是她找到责任护士。

Patient Ms. Wu, 41 years old, was hospitalized for insomnia, nervousness, anxiety and restlessness. Her symptoms of anxiety were improved after medical treatment. Her doctor had been considering reducing the dose of her sleep medicine. But the patient became very anxious and worried that she wouldn't fall asleep at night. She went to talk to her nurse.

交流 / Interactions

病人:我的病刚刚好一点,你们就要给我减药,晚上肯定睡不好,

第三部分 特殊人群(情境)沟通

毛病就会加重。这样肯定不行,你帮我跟医生讲讲,不要减药。

Patient: My doctor plans to reduce the dose of my medicine. If I don't take enough medicine, I can't sleep well and my illness will get worse. Could you help me ask the doctor not to reduce the dose of my medicine?

护士:你的心情我理解。但是,治疗是一个完整的过程,总有减药的时间。

Nurse: I understand how you feel. But the whole treatment process consists of many stages. At some point, the dosage of the medicine will need to be reduced.

病人:我知道,但现在肯定不行。

Patient: I see. But it is not the right time, yet.

护士:医生对你的病情很了解。这是根据你的病情进行的用药调整,你该信任你的床位医生。

Nurse: Your doctor knows about your condition very well. He adjusts your medication according to your condition. You should trust your doctor.

病人:我不是不相信医生,可万一减了药真的睡不着,那该怎么办?

Patient: I do trust my doctor. But I don't know what to do if I cannot sleep well at night.

护士:你放心,晚上我们的值班护士会定时巡视病房。如果你真的睡不着,她会联系值班医生给你酌情用药,第二天护士也会向你的床位医生作详细交班。所以,现在你要做的是放松自己。要知道,你的紧张焦虑情绪反而会严重影响你晚上的睡眠。

Nurse: Don't worry. The nurse on duty at night will look after you. She will call the doctor on duty to give you medication if you can't fall asleep. And she will report your condition to your doctor in detail the following morning. So now you should try to relax. As you know, your anxiety and nervousness will affect your sleep.

病人:听你这么一解释,我现在放心一点了。

Part Ⅲ Nursing Care for Special Patient Groups

Patient: I feel a little better now after your explanation.
护士:那太好了。我带你出去散散步,放松一下。
Nurse: Great. Let's take a walk to relax some.
病人:好的,谢谢你。
Patient: OK and thanks.

结果 / *Result*

由于护士给予了有效的心理疏导,病人解除了因减药而带来的焦虑情绪,整夜睡眠没有问题。

Because of the effective psychological guidance from the nurse, it reduced the patient's anxiety caused by the medicine reduction. The patient slept through the night without a problem.

点评 / *Comments*

吴女士因减药而出现焦虑,护士对其所担心的事情作出合理的解释和保证,并带其外出散步转移注意力,有效地减少了病人的焦虑情绪。

Ms. Wu was anxious due to the reduction of her medicine. According to the things that worried the patient, the nurse provided reasonable explanations and reassurance, and also took the patient out for a walk. These diverted the patient's attention and effectively reduced her anxiety.

第三部分 特殊人群(情境)沟通

神经性厌食病人的护理
Nursing Care for a Patient with Anorexia Nervosa

赵惠英

背景/ Background

高女士,大三学生,身材高挑,长相甜美,一直都是同龄女孩羡慕的对象。然而,近两个月来,突然出现厌食、闭经、体重直线下降,骨瘦如柴,只能卧床休息,个人生活也不能自理。突如其来的这些情况使她无法面对,情绪极度低落。入院后,她迫切地想恢复进食,但又无法做到,反而出现胃部不适、恶心呕吐。这时她找到责任护士,向护士求助。

Miss Gao, a junior at a university, tall and pretty, was admired by other girls of her age. But during the last two months, she couldn't eat anything, her menstruation stopped, she lost a lot of weight and she looked very thin. She had to lie in bed all day long, and couldn't do anything by herself. She could not face her current condition and was very depressed. After she was admitted to the hospital, she was eager to eat something, but she felt stomach discomfort, nausea and sometimes even vomited. She asked her primary nurse to help her.

Part III Nursing Care for Special Patient Groups

交流 / *Interactions*

病人：护士,我到底得了什么病?

Patient: What's wrong with me?

护士：你患的是"神经性厌食症"。

Nurse: You are suffering from Anorexia Nervosa.

病人：这病能治好么?

Patient: Can I recover from this disease?

护士：当然能治好,但需要你的配合。

Nurse: Sure. But we need your cooperation.

病人：现在我真的很后悔。当初为了保持自己漂亮的身材,每天都刻意减少自己的进食量,有时甚至在饭后采用自我催吐法将食物呕出。慢慢地就开始吃不下东西了,而且见到吃的东西就难受。现在甚至出现了闭经,生活都不能自理,都怨我自己。

Patient: I'm so regretful now. In order to keep my pretty figure, I reduced my eating intentionally. Sometimes I even induced vomiting after I ate. Gradually I did not want to eat anything, and had an upset stomach when I saw the food. Now my menstruation has stopped. I can't even look after myself. It is my own fault.

护士："爱美之心,人皆有之",像你这样拼命节食减肥的女孩不少。你像其他人一样,步入了减肥的误区。现在你已经意识到了健康的重要性,为时不晚呀。实际上要保持良好的身材,可以通过运动来达到,这样既锻炼了身体,又保持了健美的体型。如果只是一味地采取极端节食的话,不仅不能有效的保持自己健美的体型,反而还会损害自己的健康,得不偿失。

Nurse: Everybody loves a beautiful figure. You have stepped into a vicious circle just like lots of other girls who try to limit their eating to reduce their weight. But now you are aware of the importance of health. Actually, you can depend on exercise to keep your figure. Exercise is good for both your health and your figure. Restricting eating alone will not keep

第三部分 特殊人群(情境)沟通

your beautiful figure effectively, and it will ruin your health. It's not worthwhile.

病人: 是啊,我现在最担心的就是自己的健康,强迫自己多吃点,但是不行啊！我该怎么办呢？

Patient: Right. Now I worry about my health very much. I force myself to eat more. But it doesn't work. What should I do?

护士: 首先你要保持良好的心态,积极配合医生的各项治疗。其次,目前你严重营养不良,而且因为长期过度节食,造成了你胃肠功能紊乱,如果突然间大量进食,肯定会适得其反。所以千万不可操之过急,只能循序渐进,少食多餐,逐步增加进食量。在此基础上,再逐步增加运动量,如从在床上做简单运动伸伸腿开始,至下床走动等。总之,不要着急,要慢慢来,对自己要有信心。我相信你会慢慢地康复起来。你自己觉得呢？

Nurse: First, you should be optimistic, and accept various treatments from your doctor. Second, you are in severe malnutrition now. It is not good for you to eat large amounts of food suddenly because your gastrointestinal function has been disturbed due to long periods of restricted eating. So take it easy. You should gradually increase the amount of food, eat less each time but eat more frequently. Third, gradually increase the amount of exercise, for example, from lifting your legs on the bed to having a short walk. In a word, be patient and trust yourself. I'm sure you will recover from your illness. Do you agree with me?

病人: 我听你的,我会努力的。

Patient: I'll try my best.

结果 / Result

高女士消除了顾虑,与责任护士一起制订了合理的饮食计划和作息计划。两周后能自己下床活动,一月后能正常进食。

Miss Gao's worries have been reduced. She worked with the nurse to plan her diet, activities, and rests. After two weeks, she can take walks

Part Ⅲ Nursing Care for Special Patient Groups

by herself. After one month, she can eat normally.

点评/ *Comments*

小高非常想改变因节食而带来的严重后果,但又对自己的疾病无正确的认识。护士及时提供信息,给予专业性的指导,增强了小高对治疗的信心。

Miss Gao wanted to change the serious consequences of her dieting. But she didn't understand her illness. The nurse provided her the information timely and gave her the specialized instructions. Miss Gao gained confidence in recovering from her disease.

第三部分 特殊人群(情境)沟通

Ⅲ-12

疼痛用药的心理护理
Psychological Nursing Care for a Patient Suffering from Pain

李惠玲

背景 / Background

病人小张,男性,33 岁,因原发性肝癌侵及肝门部而入院,接受化疗。虽然化疗后无明显反应,但夜间肝区疼痛,常常使他难以忍受。医生给他开了小剂量杜冷丁,但病人怕用后成瘾而拒绝了。于是责任护士对小张说了下面这段话。

Patient Mr. Zhang, 33 years old, was admitted to the hospital for chemotherapy because of a primary liver carcinoma which had involved the portal area. He had no obvious side effects after chemotherapy, but the severe pain in his liver area at night had become unbearable. The doctor prescribed small doses of Dolantin for him. However, Mr. Zhang refused to take the pills for fear of addiction. The responsible nurse went to talk to him.

Part Ⅲ Nursing Care for Special Patient Groups

交流 / *Interactions*

护士:从您额头沁出的冷汗中,我感觉到这肝部疼痛是难以忍受的。如果是我,一定会哼出声来的,而您怕影响其他病人,忍住了。但这样将消耗您很多体力,所以我还是建议您接受适量的止痛剂。放心,小剂量的止痛剂不会有什么副作用的。

Nurse: From the cold sweat on your forehead, I can see that your liver pain is unbearable. If I were you, I wouldn't be able to keep myself from groaning. I know that you don't want to disturb other patients so you are trying to tolerate the pain silently. However, you will soon exhaust your physical strength this way. I suggest you take some analgesics. Don't worry. A small dosage of Dolantin won't cause any side effects.

病人:我不担心别的,就怕成瘾。

Patient: I'm not afraid of anything else but becoming addicted to the drugs.

护士:不会的,不用担心。我们将按"三阶梯止痛法"为你合理用药,不会有问题。希望你能同意我的意见。

Nurse: No, don't worry about it. We will appropriately use the drugs according to the "three-grade pain control method". It will not cause problems for you. I hope you will listen to me.

病人:那么让我先试试这个疗法吧。

Patient: OK. Let me try it.

护士:好的。你同意用这个疗法,让我们先试试看。

Nurse: Good. You agree to use this method. Let's try it.

第三部分　特殊人群（情境）沟通

结果 / Result

病人按"三阶梯止痛法"经适量止痛后,能安静入睡了,并以较好的身心状态接受化疗。

The patient could sleep peacefully with the "three-grade-pain control method". He went through the chemotherapy with a better mental and physical status.

Part Ⅲ   Nursing Care for Special Patient Groups

病人伤口愈合问题的心理护理
Psychological Nursing Care for a Patient with a Wound Healing Problem

徐蓉

背景/ *Background*

陆先生,73岁,因6月前胃部手术后窦道形成,由于创面长期不愈,脾气比较急躁、缺乏耐心、主观强,常对医务人员抱怨、挑剔,不合作,对各项护理和治疗配合欠佳。

Mr. Lu, 73 years old, was hospitalized due to a fistula formation after a gastric operation 6 months ago. Because of the long period of suffering from the wound, this patient became easily angered, had no patience for any treatment, always complained, and would not cooperate with nursing care and treatment.

交流/ *Interactions*

护士:陆老伯,您好! 要输液了,要上个厕所吗? 床要给你摇平吗?

Nurse: Hello, Mr. Lu. I'm going to give you an intravenous transfusion. Do you want to go to the bathroom first? Is your bed angle comforta-

第三部分 特殊人群(情境)沟通

ble for you?

病人：(半卧位)不要，就这样好了，这样我舒服。(眼睛转了几下，斜瞄了一眼正挂上去的补液袋，表情不屑和不耐)天天挂水，病又没给我挂好，钱倒花了不少。

Patient：(semireclining position) Yes, this is fine. I feel comfortable this way. (looking at the fluid bag with an unworthy and impatient expression) I receive an IV every day which costs me a lot of money, but I haven't felt any better.

护士：陆老伯，我们知道您受罪了，但是您不是一天比一天好吗？再说，这病情的好转也是需要一定时间的，今天换药时我看了您的伤口，愈合得很好。

Nurse：Well, Mr. Lu, I know you are suffering, but you are getting better every day. The treatment needs time. I have just examined your wound. It's getting better.

病人：(表情很恼火，嘴里不时地嘟哝)需要时间！我反反复复多久了，这个看看，那个治治，一直到了现在。

Patient：(angrily complaining) Needs time! Back and forth, I'm treated by a different person. Do you know how long I've suffered from this?

护士：(改变话题)今天早饭吃什么了，胃口好吗(同时进行输液的各个步骤)？

Nurse：(changing the subject) What did you have for breakfast this morning? How was your appetite (preparing the transfusion at the same time)?

病人：胃口？还提什么胃口！我什么都吃不下去！(头转向窗外，发出一声叹息。)

Patient：Appetite? Don't mention it. I can't eat anything. (He turned his head toward the window and sighed.)

护士：这可不太好！其实饮食对创面的修复很重要，那您是什么都不想吃呢还是觉得咽不下去？好，请握一下拳，要准备注射了，稍微有点感觉啊，请忍忍！看您这胳膊细的，你一定得吃点东西！

Part III Nursing Care for Special Patient Groups

Nurse: That's not good! Nutrition is very important for healing of the wound. Do you not have an appetite for anything or can't you just swallow it? Look, your arm is so thin. You must eat something. Please make a fist. I'm going to insert the needle now. This will hurt a little. Please try to hold still for a moment.

病人:(双眉紧皱)唉!这么长时间了,又不吃什么,怎么会不瘦?(瞄了一眼在给他安置针的护士)今天挂什么?有没有血浆、蛋白?

Patient: (frowning) Well, it's been a long time since I've not been eating. How can I not be getting thinner? (taking a look at the nurse who is stabilizing the needle) What are you going to give me today, blood or albumin?

护士:有的,因为您吃得少,摄入量不够,我们必须采取一定的治疗方法来补补您的身体。

Nurse: Yes. You have not been eating much, so you have not had enough intake of calories. We have to take a treatment strategy to keep you in proper condition with some nutrition.

病人:(摇摇头)一千块钱又要没有了!这病怎么看得起哟!

Patient: (shaking his head) It will cost me another 1,000 yuan today. How am I going to pay for this?

护士:是的,现在的医疗费用是不低,所以呀,老话说"药补不如食补",您还不如多吃点,就不多花买药的钱了,您如果胃口不好,可以改善进食的种类、质量,增加花样,也可向医生反映,使用健胃药物辅助,如咽不下去,可以作进一步的检查,查明原因,不能总是这样吧,您说呢?

Nurse: The costs of medical expenses are not low. Therefore, the truth is: it's better to take food instead of medication. You should eat more, then you won't need to spend so much money on medicine. Why not eat more nutritional food? This will decrease your costs. If your appetite is not good, we can increase the variety and improve the quality of the food. You can also tell the doctor to see if they can do something for you if you

第三部分 特殊人群(情境)沟通

have difficulty swallowing the food.

病人:(眉头紧皱,但语气有缓和)那我该吃什么呢?

Patient:(frowning and speaking with an easier tone) What kind of food should I eat?

(护士作了相关饮食与营养方面的宣教,并表示会再次与家属沟通。)

(The nurse explained diet and nutrition related information and expressed willingness to further communicate with his family members.)

病人:知道了,你走吧,等我女儿、儿子来了再说,我要歇会了。对了,把医生给我叫来,我有事呢!

Patient: I know. Please leave me alone. I want to have a rest before my daughter and my son arrive. By the way, please call the doctor for me.

护士:噢,他们可能在手术,不一定在,我去看看,我能帮您转达吗?

Nurse: The doctors are performing an operation right now. I will inform them as soon as possible. Can I take a message for you?

病人:(态度很不耐烦)不用,我自己问,等有空了再说。不要忘了,不要一天见不到人。

Patient:(impatient) No, thank you. I will ask the doctor myself. Wait till he has time to come. Please don't disappear from me all the time.

护士:好的,您好好休息,我一定转告他们。我过一会再来看您,好吗?

Nurse: OK, have a rest. I will inform them and see you a little bit later.

(病人点头表示同意,半卧位,眼睛微闭。)

(The patient nodded his head indicating agreement on semireclining position, eyes closed.)

点评/ Comments

在临床的护理工作中,护士会遇到有些病人由于病程时间长等多

Part III Nursing Care for Special Patient Groups

种原因造成厌烦情绪，出现不合作或反常行为。作为护理人员，要理解病人，充分移情，换位思考，同情体谅他们。避免感情用事，要巧用多种方式减少矛盾。

During the clinical nursing work, nurses will meet some patients with an impatient, uncooperative attitude, or with abnormal behavior due to their long-term illness. Nurses should understand what has happened to them, put their feet in the patients' shoes, and be kind and compassionate to them. They should avoid emotional reactions, and use strategies to reduce the conflict.

第三部分 特殊人群(情境)沟通

五、家庭、社会或文化有关问题的护理
Nursing Care for Patients with Family, Social or Culture Related Problems

关切自我形象
Concerning Self-image

王稚

背景 / Background

病人,刘老太太,70岁,高级知识分子,因患脑出血住院两周。因平时养成良好的卫生习惯,故卧床两周未洗头,自感不舒适,自行起床洗头。护士小陈对病人进行了正确的护理引导。

Patient Mrs. Liu, a 70 year-old intellectual, was hospitalized for two weeks because of a cerebral hemorrhage. Because of her good hygiene habits, she felt very uncomfortable not washing her hair for two weeks. She decided to get up to wash her hair. Nurse Chen came to talk to the patient.

交流 / Interactions

病人:睡了一个多星期了,每天护工阿姨给我擦两次身,这身上的感觉倒还可以。就是这头发,我自己都能闻到酸臭味了,摸上去腻腻的,真是难受死了!

Part Ⅲ　Nursing Care for Special Patient Groups

Patient：I have been resting in bed for more than a week. The nursing assistant gave me a bed-bath twice every day. So my body feels OK, but my hair is awful. It smells and feels greasy. I feel awful.

病人老伴：让我摸摸你的头发,还好啊。现在可是生病的非常时期啊,你可不能像平时那样讲究了。

Patient's Husband：Let me touch your hair. It's not so bad. You are sick and you can't be as trendy as before.

病人：唉,要是女儿在身边就好了,让她给我洗一洗,多贴心啊。

Patient：Alas, if only my daughter could be here. I would have asked her to wash my hair.

病人老伴：要不让护工阿姨给你洗一洗吧。

Patient's Husband：Would you like to ask the nursing assistant to wash your hair?

（此时护士小陈巡视到病人床边,看到刘阿婆及陪护工人正忙活着要洗头,赶忙上前制止。）

(At that time Nurse Chen made her rounds to the ward and saw the nursing assistant about to wash Mrs. Liu's hair. So she walked up to stop them.)

护士：刘阿婆,您患的是脑出血,现在还处于急性期,需要严格卧床休息,千万可不能洗头,引起再出血,可不是闹着玩的。

Nurse：Mrs. Liu, you are suffering from a cerebral hemorrhage. It's still in the acute stage. You need to be on strict bed rest and absolutely can't wash your hair. Bleeding again would be serious.

病人：可是我的头实在是太脏了,我真的快要受不了了！

Patient：But my hair is too dirty. I can't stand it any more.

护士：您别着急,我早就替您想好了。等过了这个星期,我会用洗头机给您在床上洗头,您一点也不用麻烦,躺在床上就可以了。

Nurse：Don't worry. I have already planned it for you. After this week, I will use the hair washing machine to wash your hair in bed. It will have no trouble at all.

第三部分 特殊人群(情境)沟通

病人老伴:那真是太好了!老伴啊,你就再忍一忍吧!
Patient's Husband: That will be great! Darling, please endure it a little longer.

(过了几天,床位护士小陈推着洗头机来到了阿婆床边。)
(A few days later, Nurse Chen pushed the hair washing machine to Mrs. Liu' bedside.)

护士:刘阿婆,我来给您洗头了。我把这个头托给您垫上,您就睡在这个头托上就可以了,一会就好了。
Nurse: Mrs. Liu, I'm here to wash your hair now. Put this pad under your head. Lie down on the pad and it will only take a minute.

(温热的水,徐徐地流出。护士小陈轻轻地揉搓着阿婆的头发,一遍遍地清洗干净。)
(With warm water slowly pouring, Nurse Chen kneaded the elder's hair gently and rinsed her hair once and again.)

病人:真好啊,太舒服了,太谢谢你了,陈小姐。
Patient: How nice and comfortable. Miss Chen, thank you very much.

护士:没事,不用谢我。别急,还有最后一道工序呢!
Nurse: You are welcome. Now take it easy. There's one more step to do.

(正说着,小陈拿出吹风机慢慢吹干阿婆的头发,用梳子梳整齐了,并拿出镜子给阿婆照了照。)
(Nurse Chen took out a hair dryer and dried the patient's hair slowly, combed her hair with a comb, and took out a mirror and let the patient see her hair.)

护士:好了,阿婆,您看您多精神啊!
Nurse: Well, Mrs. Liu, see how nice you look now.

病人老伴:来来来,陈小姐我们一起来合个影吧。我要把照片寄给我在澳大利亚的女儿看看,让她也放心。既使她不在我们身边,但这儿也有像女儿一样的护士小姐照顾着我们。

Part Ⅲ Nursing Care for Special Patient Groups

Patient's Husband: Come here, Miss Chen. Take a picture with us. I will send it to my daughter in Australia. Let her not worry. Although she is not here with us, we have the nurse like a daughter here to take care of us.

点评/ Comments

基础护理是临床工作的重点,为老年患者提供优质的护理尤为重要。目前,越来越多的空巢老人因孤独而渴望得到子女们的关爱。通过护理人员悉心的护理和亲人般的关怀,让老年人重新体会到自身价值的所在,体会到护理工作最温柔的一面。

Basic nursing is the foundation for nursing practice. Providing excellent nursing care for older patients is especially important. These days, more and more elder people live alone. They miss the care and love from their sons and daughters very much. By paying special attention to them like their own relatives, nursing can make them realize their self-value again and recognize the tenderness of the nursing care.

第三部分　特殊人群(情境)沟通

社交障碍病人的护理
Nursing Care for a Patient with Impaired Social Interaction

赵惠英

背景/ Background

程某,男性,未婚,银行职员,工作一向认真负责,但近两个月却不愿去上班了。父母了解后得知,最近一段时间他因害羞而不敢和女孩交往的现象越来越严重,现在一看到异性就面红耳赤,紧张焦虑,甚至于在单位里连熟悉的女同事也无法面对,影响工作。父母不得已将其送入医院。程某虽然求治心切,但同时也痛苦万分,因为他一见到女护士就紧张。这天,责任护士走到了他的床边。

Mr. Cheng, a single banker, is a hard-working and highly responsible person, but he has not wanted to go to work for two months. His parents found out that he was shy when communicating with women and felt nervous and anxious. He couldn't even work with his female colleagues. His parents sent him to the hospital for treatment. Although the patient was eager to be cured, he was also very nervous to see the female nurses. His responsible nurse came to his bedside to talk to him.

Part Ⅲ　Nursing Care for Special Patient Groups

交流/ *Interactions*

护士：从你现在低垂的眼神和不停搓手的举动中,我能感觉到你面对我时的紧张不安。

Nurse: I sense you are very nervous and anxious now. You are looking down and rubbing your hands.

病人：(没抬眼)我也不知道。反正特别怕与女性接触,特别是年轻的,我会心慌、胸闷、透不过气来,我不敢看你。

Patient: (still looking down) I don't know. I'm afraid of communicating with women, especially young ladies. I have palpitations, dyspnea, and choking. I dare not look at you.

护士：你内心的痛苦和挣扎我能理解。如果我是你,处在这样的境况下,可能也会和你一样的。我的孩子比你小不了几岁。你能看一看我,彼此熟悉一下吗?

Nurse: I can understand your pain and struggle. If I were you, I probably would have the same feelings. I have a son who's not much younger than you. Can you try looking at me so we can get acquainted better?

(病人眼神在护士身上很快掠过。)

(The patient looked at the nurse quickly, then looked down again.)

护士：感觉怎么样?

Nurse: How do you feel?

病人：紧张,不敢看。

Patient: Nervous. I'm afraid to look at you.

护士：我是你的责任护士,以后你每天都会见到我。事实上,今天你已经勇敢地跨出了第一步,我很高兴。我们可以试着采用循序渐进的接触方式。请放心,这种接触方式不会使你太难受。每次只要像今天这样进步一点点,假以时日你就会发现自己已迈出了一大步。但是在此之前,我想知道你愿意和我们一起与病魔作斗争么?

Nurse: I'm your nurse. You will see me every day. I'm glad you took the first step for treatment today. We can communicate with each other in

第三部分 特殊人群(情境)沟通

an orderly way, step by step. Don't worry. This strategy should not make you very uncomfortable. Every day, you should find that you have made some progress. Do you have the will to fight your condition with us?

病人:我信任你们,知道你们是在帮助我。我也非常希望自己恢复健康,能够正常地与异性交往,但是我担心我做不到。

Patient: I trust you. I know you want to help me. I hope I can learn to communicate with women just like other men. But I'm not sure if I will succeed.

护士:不用担心,我们将按照"系统脱敏"的原则,为你制定相应的方案。相信不会有太大的难度,希望你能接受我的建议。

Nurse: Don't worry. We will make a plan for you according to the principles of systematic desensitization therapy. It will not be very hard for you. I hope you can accept my suggestion.

病人:好吧,我会好好配合的。

Patient: OK. I will cooperate.

结果 / Result

按照责任护士制定的"系统脱敏"方案实施后,慢慢地患者能与护士自然交流,并逐步能与其他异性进行正常交往。最后病人康复出院,恢复正常工作。

Gradually, the patient learned to communicate with the nurse and interact with other women without any nervousness or anxiety after going through the systematic desensitization therapy. He was discharged, and resumed his work without further problems.

Part Ⅲ　Nursing Care for Special Patient Groups

悲哀疏导
Counseling on Grieving

李惠玲

背景 / Background

相爱了40年的教授夫妇，形影相伴的情形常为人们所羡慕。然而3天前，教授北上讲学不幸飞机失事而遇难。这突如其来的打击使教授夫人无法承受，她不能进食，无法入眠，生活的天平失去了平衡，她因精神崩溃而被送入医院。这时，责任护士像女儿一般来到了她身边。

A professor couple is admired by many for their love and dedication to each other for over 40 years. Tragically, the husband was killed in a plane crash three days earlier while on his way to give a lecture. The professor's wife was having difficulty coping with the tragedy. She couldn't eat during the day and couldn't sleep at night. Her peaceful happy life seemed lost and she was on the verge of a nervous breakdown. She was admitted to the hospital. A nurse tended to her like a daughter.

交流 / Interactions

护士：夫人，我想如果您先生知道您现在这个样子，一定会很难过的。九泉之下，他会一直牵挂着您，您能忍心让他难过吗？

Nurse: Madam, I think that your husband would be very sad if he

第三部分 特殊人群(情境)沟通

knew how you were now. He would be very worried about you. Are you willing to make him sad?

(夫人沉默,悲哀地……)

(The professor's wife kept silent and sad…)

(护士坐下,轻轻地握住夫人的手,轻轻地抚摸,像女儿一般,约2分钟。)

(The nurse sat down, held the patient's hand, and stroked it gently like a daughter for two minutes.)

护士:您看,您的手冰凉,手指都凹陷了。如果还不吃东西,您会挺不住的。您的儿子给您炖了鸡汤,还热着呢,喝一点,好吗?

Nurse: Your hands are cold and thin. If you don't eat, you'll become even weaker. Your son cooked this chicken soup for you and it is still warm. Please have some, OK?

夫人:喝不下(泪水涌出眼眶)。

Professor's Wife: I don't want to eat (tears streaming from her eyes).

护士:是的,您没胃口。可您儿子为了炖这锅汤熬了几个小时,别让他太失望好吗? 来,我喂您!

Nurse: I understand you have no appetite. But your son has spent several hours cooking this soup for you. Please don't disappoint him, OK? Come on, I'll feed you.

夫人:(张开了嘴,一口一口地慢慢咽下,喝了几口后,对护士说)小姐,谢谢你,我过会儿再喝,行吗?

Professor's Wife: (She opened her mouth and had some of the chicken soup slowly. After a few bites, she said to the nurse) Thank you, Miss. I'll have some more later, OK?

护士:好的,过一会儿我再来。

Nurse: OK, I'll come back later.

(晚上8点,值班护士又来到夫人床边。)

(At eight o'clock that evening, the evening shift nurse on duty went to the patient's bedside.)

护士:夫人,日班护士告诉我您今天几乎没有吃任何东西。我为

Part Ⅲ Nursing Care for Special Patient Groups

您煮了杯牛奶,喝点好吗?

Nurse:The day shift nurse told me that you only ate a little today. I have warmed a glass of milk for you. Would you like to have some?

(夫人摇摇头。)

(The professor's wife shook her head.)

护士:夫人,我知道此刻任何安慰的话都不能使教授复生。可是,如果您能努力地打起精神为教授完成他所未完成的心愿和工作,那么教授依然会伴着您。他所翻过的书页,他所执持的笔墨,仍然由您继续发挥作用。您想,那样教授不是永远和您相伴吗?所以,从现在起您不仅仅为自己活着,而是为您和教授共同活着。

Nurse:I know that no matter what we do, it won't bring your husband back. However, if you can keep up your spirits, and help fulfill the work and ideas that remain unfinished, you will feel that he's still with you. Your husband's spirit will always be there for you. From now on you need to live not only for yourself, but also to keep his work and spirit alive.

夫人:(渐渐地,护士使夫人看到了希望。几分钟后,她接过护士手中的水杯,慢慢地、一口一口地将牛奶饮尽。)

(Gradually, the nurse aroused hope in the patient. After a few minutes, the patient took the glass and drank the milk slowly.)

结果 / Result

两周后,经过护士的理解、交谈和鼓励,运用各种非语言交流,夫人渐渐地恢复了正常的生活。她找到责任护士,告诉她自己将会好好地珍惜生命,努力去追求和实现她与教授共同的心愿和事业。

After two weeks, with the nurse's support and encouragement, the professor's wife gradually resumed her normal life. She told the nurse that she would take good care of herself and try to further pursue their common ideas to complete their unfinished work.

第三部分 特殊人群(情境)沟通

六、临床带教
Clinical Nursing Instruction

整装待发实习
Getting Ready for Nursing Practicum

杨晓莉　刘琦

时间：早晨 7:30　　　　　地点：护士站
Time：7:30 AM　　　　　 Place：Nurse Station

背景/ *Background*

在学校已学习过护士职业服饰规范的护生第一次去临床见习。护生在病区交接班前整理仪容仪表。

It was the first time for the student nurses to do clinical practice. They had already learned about the dress codes for nurses in school. The student nurses were checking their appearance before the shift change in the unit.

交流/ *Interactions*

学生：我们可以化妆吗？
Student：Can we put on make-up?

教师：当然可以。护士将内心的美与外在的美融为一体，并创造出美的环境，才能使病人感受到生命与生活的美好，从而产生战胜疾

Part Ⅲ　Nursing Care for Special Patient Groups

病的勇气。

Teacher: Of course. If nurses can combine their outward beauty with their inward beauty and create a beautiful environment, it will make the patients feel life is so beautiful and have the courage to fight against the diseases.

学生:我们应该化怎样的妆呢?

Student: What kind of make-up should we put on?

教师:清新、淡雅的妆容比较适合护士的职业。不能浓妆艳抹,留长指甲。发型一般为短发或盘发,长发要上挽,前刘海不得过眼。

Teacher: Fresh and light make-up is suitable for nurses. It's not proper for nurses to put on heavy make-up, or keep long fingernails. Generally, the hair style should be short or worn in a bun or coiled up. Hair bangs must be above the eyes.

学生:可以涂指甲油吗?

Student: Can we paint our nails?

教师:有色的指甲油是不允许的,包括趾甲油。现在有一些无色透明有营养作用的指甲油是可以的。护士也需要注重双手的保养,有一双柔软、干净、美丽的双手,不仅能带给病人娴熟的护理服务,还可以带给病人愉悦、满足的感受。

Teacher: Colorful nail polish is not permitted. This includes toenail polish. Transparent and neutral nail polish is OK. Nurses should take good care of their hands. Their hands should be soft, clean and elegant. A beautiful hand can bring the patients not only skillful services but also pleasant and satisfactory feelings.

学生:张老师,这块玉是我们家祖传的,奶奶说是我的护身符,出生以来从没有离过身,现在我能继续佩戴它吗?

Student: Miss Zhang, this jade is handed down from my ancestors. My grandma told me it was my lucky charm. I have been wearing it since I was born. Can I continue to wear it?

教师:你可以继续佩戴它,只要注意不露于衣领外面,不影响操作

第三部分 特殊人群(情境)沟通

就行了。

Teacher: Yes, you can wear it as long as it won't get out of your shirt collar and won't hinder your work.

学生:好的,我会注意的。

Student: OK, I know.

结果/ Result

学生在教师的指导下不仅学会了护士的职业仪容仪表规范,也感受到了临床实际工作中的人性化管理。

With the direction of the teacher, the student nurses not only learned the appearance standards for nurses but also felt the humanistic management in practice.

点评/ Comments

教师与护生之间的对话简洁明了,充满人性化。对护生的仪容仪表要求体现了心灵美和外表美的和谐统一。

The dialogue between the teacher and the student nurses is very concise and with humanity. The requirements for appearance are a real manifestation of the harmonious combination of inward and outward beauty.

Part III Nursing Care for Special Patient Groups

测量体温示教
Demonstration of Body Temperature Measuring Technique

杨晓莉   刘琦

教师:小芳,现在是测量体温的时间了。我和你一起去好吗?

Teacher: Xiao Fang, it's time to take temperatures. Shall we go together?

学生:好的。我已准备好要用的物品:体温计、记录本、笔、润滑油和浸有消毒液的纱布。

Student: OK. I have prepared the following: thermometer, notebook, pen, lubricating oil and gauze soaked with disinfectant.

教师:还应带什么?

Teacher: What else should you take?

学生:手表。

Student: A watch.

教师:为什么?

Teacher: Why?

第三部分 特殊人群(情境)沟通

学生:在测量体温的同时,需要为病人测量脉搏,观察呼吸的频率,因此,手表是这项操作的必备工具。

Student: We need to take the patient's pulse and observe the respiratory rate while taking the temperature. So a watch is needed.

教师:很好。能告诉我你是怎样准备体温计的吗?

Teacher: Very good. Could you tell me how to prepare the thermometer?

学生:检查体温计是否完好,看水银柱是否在35℃以下。

Student: Check the thermometer to see if it is in good condition. The mercury column should be below 35℃.

教师:好,让我们一起去吧。

Teacher: Good. Let's go.

学生:好的。

Student: OK.

学生:刘先生,今天感觉怎么样?

Student: Mr. Liu, how do you feel today?

病人:还不错,比昨天好多了。

Patient: Not too bad. Better than yesterday.

教师:您刚才喝水了吗?有没有吃东西?

Teacher: Did you drink water or eat something just now?

病人:没有。

Patient: No.

教师:刚才洗澡了吗?

Teacher: Did you just take a bath?

病人:也没有。为什么要问这些?

Patient: No. Why do you ask?

教师:如果刚喝水、就餐和沐浴,都将影响测量数据的准确性。如

Part III Nursing Care for Special Patient Groups

果有,我们将过30分钟再为您测量。

Teacher: Your temperature reading would be inaccurate if you drank water, had a meal or took a bath just before taking the temperature. If so, we'll take your temperature in 30 minutes.

病人:哦,我懂了。

Patient: Oh, I see.

学生:请您张开嘴,卷起舌头,这样有助于我将体温表放在正确的位置。请放平舌头,闭口3分钟。

Student: Please open your mouth and put the thermometer under your tongue. Please close your mouth for 3 minutes.

学生:请将手伸出来,手掌朝上,我再为您测量脉搏。

Student: Please stretch out a hand with the palm up and let me measure your pulse.

(3分钟后)

(3 minutes later.)

学生:好了,体温36.9℃,脉搏78次/分,呼吸20次/分,一切正常。谢谢您的合作!

Student: OK. Your temperature is 36.9℃, pulse is 78 b/m, and respiration is 20 t/m. All are normal. Thanks for your cooperation.

点评 / Comments

在护理体检中加强人际沟通,多用安慰、解释、鼓励的语言。当病人提出各种问题时,应用婉转的语调耐心地解释。如文中所示,运用耐心的解释性语言既解除了病人的思想顾虑和负担,满足其心理需要,又进行了健康宣教。教师给护生角色示教,既示范操作又施教沟通,达到了整体护理的示范效果。

During a physical check-up, it is better to use consolatory, explana-

第三部分 特殊人群(情境)沟通

tory and encouraging words. When answering the patient's questions, a nurse should speak in a tactful tone, and give explanations patiently. As in this example, tactful and explanatory words have not only relieved the patient's anxieties and worries and met his psychological needs, but also played a very good role in health education. The teacher is a role model for the student. After the teacher's on-the-spot demonstration and communication skill training, the effect of holistic nursing is achieved.

附录 Appendix

安宁照护
Hospice Care

李惠玲

背景/ Background

蒋先生因患晚期肝癌生命垂危，进入了临终状态。这几天他情绪极低，一直在自责自己没能及时进行每年体检以致病入膏肓。因为病痛和虚弱，医生给他开了绝对卧床休息的医嘱，用白蛋白支持，小剂量吗啡镇痛。蒋先生病前是公司白领，平时很注重个人卫生清洁，这次入院由于虚弱，他已经一个月没洗澡了，身上皮肤黄疸搔痒难忍，夫人很想帮他洗澡，但是不敢。这天，他终于忍不住了，坚决要求护士长帮忙给他洗澡。但这时，他的血压较低，极其虚弱，护士长汇报医生后未果，只好拨通护理部主任的电话求助。这时，主任来到了蒋先生床边。

Mr. Jiang was terminally ill with advanced-stage liver cancer. He had been in low spirits these days and had been blaming himself for having not taken the yearly physical examination in time. Because he was in great pain and felt weak, the doctor had prescribed him absolute bed rest, albumin support and pain management with a small dose of morphine. Mr. Jiang used to be a white-collar, so he paid much attention to personal hygiene. During his hospitalization this time, he hadn't taken a shower for one month because of weakness. Jaundice appeared on his skin and he was

附录　安宁照护

suffering from unbearable itch. Mrs. Jiang would like very much to give him a bath but she dare not. He could no longer bear the itch today and insisted that the head nurse give him a bath, but his blood pressure was rather low and he was extremely weak at this moment. The head nurse reported to the doctor but got no response, so she had to phone the superintendent of Nursing Department for help. Upon this, the superintendent came to Mr. Jiang's bedside.

交流 / Interactions

护理部主任:(走到床边,轻轻拉开蒋先生的衣袖,看了看,黄黄的胳膊上面全是手指搔痒的划痕)您很想洗澡,是吗？一个月没冲淋了,如果是我也会熬不住的。(转向蒋夫人)夫人也想帮他洗是吗？

Superintendent of Nursing Department: (He came to the bedside, gently pulled up Mr. Jiang's sleeve and saw that his yellow arm was covered with marks of scratching by fingers.) You would like to take a bath very much, right? You haven't had a shower for one month. If I were you, I also couldn't bear it. (turning to Mrs. Jiang) You wanted to give him a bath, didn't you, Ma'am?

蒋夫人:是的,就是不敢。

Mrs. Jiang: Yes, but I dare not.

护理部主任:(摸了下蒋先生的脉搏,看看监护仪的血压、氧饱和参数,基本在正常范围,对护士长说)请床位医生护驾,准备好抢救车和氧气装置,还有吸引器。(转向蒋夫人)蒋夫人,我们准备和您一起帮他洗澡,需要您签个字,洗澡的过程可能存在呕血、休克等危险,我们将共同承担责任,可以吗？

Superintendent: (He felt Mr. Jiang's pulse, looked at the blood pressure reading and oxygen saturation parameter on the monitor which were close to the normal range, and said to the head nurse.) Please ask the doctor in charge to come to help, get the resuscitation cart, oxygen unit and suction ready. (turning to Mrs. Jiang) Mrs. Jiang, we are going to

Appendix Hospice Care

assist you in bathing your husband and we need you to sign here because there might be risks of hematemesis or shock during the bathing process. We will shoulder the responsibility together. Is that acceptable?

蒋夫人:(点点头,在病历上签了字。)

Mrs. Jiang: (She nodded and signed on her husband's chart.)

护理部主任:护士长、床位护士和我还有夫人,我们共同帮他洗澡。由于患者较虚弱,只有10分钟时间,我们需要在浴缸内放好椅子等所有防护设备。蒋先生,我们都是你的妹妹,你不介意我们帮您洗澡吧?您夫人替您洗下半身,我们替您洗上半身,如何?

Superintendent: Ma'am, the head nurse, the nurse in charge and I are going to give him a bath. Since he is rather weak, he can only bathe for 10 minutes. We need to place all the protective devices such as a chair in the bathtub. Mr. Jiang, all of us are your younger sisters, so I hope you wouldn't mind our giving you a bath. Your wife will bathe the lower half of your body and we will take care of the upper half. What do you think?

蒋先生:(点头)谢谢你了!

Mr. Jiang: (nodding) Thank you!

护理部主任:好了,让我们调好水温和室温,开始吧!蒋先生,我先要冲湿您的头发,哦,水温刚好,您试试行吗?(边说边和护士长、床位护士共同给他用洗发香波揉搓他的头发)这样会不会太重?有什么不舒服请告诉我好吗?

Superintendent: Well, let's regulate the water temperature and room temperature and get started! Mr. Jiang, I am going to wet your hair with the nozzle first. The water temperature is just right. Would you like to feel it? (using shampoo to knead his hair with the help of the head nurse and the nurse in charge) Is this too hard? If you feel any discomfort, please feel free to tell me, OK?

蒋先生:太舒服了,觉得很轻松。(他的夫人用毛巾帮他搓着下身。约10分钟,屋里弥漫着洗发和沐浴露的芳香。)

附录　安宁照护

Mr. Jiang: It's so comfortable and relaxing! (His wife used a towel to clean the lower part of his body. About 10 minutes had passed and the room was filled with the fragrance of shampoo and body wash.)

护理部主任:(看了眼墙上的时钟)时间到了。(搭了下蒋先生的脉搏每分钟 112 次)不能再洗了,马上停止吧!

Superintendent: (taking a look at the clock on the wall) Time is up. (feeling Mr. Jiang's pulse and it was 112 t/m) You cannot bathe any longer! Stop right now!

蒋先生:再让我冲一会儿吧,舒服极了,我好像感到自己又活回来了……

Mr. Jiang: Let me shower for a little longer. It's extremely comfortable and I feel revived…

护理部主任:蒋先生,您的脉搏在加速,头上在出汗,不能再冲了,否则血管继续扩张会休克的,现在需要休息。来,我们用大毛巾将您裹起来,头也要用干毛巾裹一下,否则会着凉感冒的。

Superintendent: Mr. Jiang, your pulse is accelerating and you are sweating on the head. You can't shower any longer otherwise your blood vessels will dilate, which will lead to shock. You need to take a rest now. Come here, we are going to wrap you up with this large towel. Your head will also be wrapped up with a dry towel or else you would catch a cold.

护士长(护士长、床位医生、护士及家属共同将他抱回轮椅,推回病床。护士长用吹风机给蒋先生吹头发,其他人则帮助他擦干身体,穿上干净的衣服。)您现在感觉如何?是否很累?

Head Nurse: (The head nurse, doctor in charge, nurse in charge and the patient's family together carried him to his wheelchair and pushed him back to his bedside. The head nurse used a hair dryer to dry Mr. Jiang's hair and the others helped wipe his body dry and change to clean clothes.) How are you feeling now? Are you very tired?

蒋先生:真的很舒服,能够在这个时候洗上澡,我死而无憾了!

Mr. Jiang: Very comfortable indeed. Being able to take a bath at this

Appendix　Hospice Care

moment of my life, I will die without any regret!

点评/ Comments

有效沟通

1. 鼓励患者宣泄不良情绪,帮助患者解除心中顾虑。
2. 有准备地接受死亡,完成生前遗嘱。
3. 尽力满足患者和家人在患者临终前的需要,不留下遗憾。
4. 让患者感受人间真情,获得社会人的完整并被尊重。

无效沟通

1. 患者的情绪得不到抒发,不能真实地宣泄和表达自己。
2. 患者没有勇气面对疾病和死亡,回避谈死亡。
3. 患者及家人对突如其来的死亡局面茫然而绝望,无力应对。
4. 患者临终前感到措手不及,憾然离世。

注意事项

1. 评估患者要全面,注意患者及家属的个性心理需求。
2. 关注患者生理、心理、社会、家庭及宗教文化信仰等整体需求,尽力满足临终者最后的身心各方面整体需求。
3. 临终濒死者会有某种程度的消沉和抑郁,更多的期望在家中离去。应在充分评估的基础上,尽力满足他们的这种需求。
4. 即使在生命弥留之际,也要注意保护患者的隐私,尊重患者的意愿,但有时会遇到法律、责任、义务、伦理等方面的冲突,作为护理管理者必须充分考量医护、护患等各方面因素。

Effective Communication

1. Encourage patients to vent negative emotions, which will help remove their worries.

2. Prepare to accept death and complete a living will.

3. Try best to meet the needs of patients and their families in order not to leave any regret.

4. Show true feelings for patients, provide them with a sense of integrity as a social being and respect them.

附录 安宁照护

Ineffective Communication

1. Patients' emotions cannot be vented and they cannot express themselves truly.

2. Patients have no courage to face the disease and death and avoid mentioning death.

3. Patients and their families feel at a loss, desperate and unable to cope.

4. Patients are unprepared for the death and leave with regrets.

Cautions

1. Give patients a comprehensive assessment and pay attention to their and their families' individual psychological needs.

2. Take care of patients' physiological, psychological, social, family, religious and cultural needs as a whole and try best to meet the last integral physical and mental needs of the dying.

3. The terminally ill will develop depression to some extent and the majority of them wish to die at home. Do our best to satisfy such needs on the basis of full assessment.

4. Protect patients' privacy and respect their wishes even when they are dying. However, sometimes when in conflict with laws, responsibilities, obligations and ethics, nursing managers should take doctor-nurse and nurse-patient aspects into full consideration.